(W)56-10159
3-18-57

American Politics in a Revolutionary World

THE GODKIN LECTURES AT HARVARD
UNIVERSITY, 1956

American Politics in a Revolutionary World

Chester Bowles

HARVARD UNIVERSITY PRESS
CAMBRIDGE

1956

The Godkin Lectures on the Essentials of Free Government and the Duties of the Citizen were established at Harvard University in memory of Edwin Lawrence Godkin (1831–1902).

Foreword

In the spring of 1956 America's attention is already focused on the important decision to be made in November. This election occurs in a particularly crucial period, in which our influence, welfare, security, and the principles on which our democratic society is based are facing the most formidable challenge in our history.

Yet with all its tumult and confusion, the debate now in progress reflects, by and large, no special sense of urgency. The issues on which we appear destined to pass judgment have the comfortable, familiar ring of easier and less dangerous days.

How can this be explained? Why do so many political leaders of both parties seem reluctant to come to grips with the new, fundamental, pressing questions of our age?

There may be many reasons: the issues are unfamiliar and complex; their full implications can still

be seen only dimly; political habits and loyalties are
well established; the new developments refuse easily
to fit into current political alignments.

Yet I believe a vague sense of unease is developing among many millions of Americans, a restless
questing for something that will give meaning and
purpose to their politics, commensurate with the
urgent new problems which they sense lie all around
us.

On three previous occasions the American people
have come up against new situations which no longer
responded to the slogans and political approaches
which had been created for an earlier day. On each
of these occasions their response has been brilliantly
effective, and we have moved into a new period of
creative growth.

Unless I am profoundly mistaken, a similar situation is developing today, out of which a new political
and economic liberalism will ultimately take shape.
As in 1800, 1861, and 1932, the American people are
again starting to blink away their self-complacency,
and to grope for a more positive role to play in a
world that cries for a reassertion of their country's
greatness.

The full dimensions of that role, its precise direction and timetable of development remain to be
shaped by events, but even more by the emergence
of political leaders who offer their fellow citizens

a new sense of national purpose, and a domestic and world-wide program of action that boldly reflects that purpose.

There are few who will argue seriously that either party as such has yet offered such leadership. Yet only those who are blind to our creativeness, resilience, and deep belief in fundamental human values will assume that America will not ultimately emerge from its present confusion and apathy, and, in the context of today's revolutionary world, rededicate its efforts to the preservation and extension of those values not only at home but abroad.

The theory of political evolution with which these pages are concerned has developed out of my reading of American history, my firsthand observation of our two political parties in action, and thousands of talks with fellow citizens in all walks of life in most of our forty-eight states.

Although I lay no claim to professional standing as either a historian or politician, I believe there is a solid element of truth, if not prophecy, in what I have tried to say.

Chester Bowles
Essex, Connecticut
April 18, 1956

Contents

American Politics in a
Revolutionary World

I

A Theory of Political Development

In this election year the attention of most Americans will be focused on the prospects of our two political parties. A study of long-term political cycles may seem, therefore, academic and beside the point.

Yet I believe that a consideration of these cycles will give us greater insight into the nature of our present alignments, help us to judge more accurately the validity of current arguments, and even suggest, after a fashion, the course of our political development in the years ahead.

Any attempt to deal briefly with American political history is an exercise in selectivity. The comforting consequence is that one need not insist on the validity of his own analysis for all times and purposes. Events and relationships will be differently stressed by different people according to their interests and points of view and according to the purposes for which they make their analysis.

My purpose is to consider whether and how our system can mobilize the creative political resources to deal effectively with the demands of the explosive new time in which we live. I believe that to do so may require rather fundamental shifting and rearrangement in the present political alignment, not only of our two parties but in the deeper strata of public attitudes which support and maintain them. I shall concentrate, therefore, on the times and manner of such creative political responses in our past, even though this leads me to neglect other features of our political processes which are less relevant for my present purpose.

From this point of view American political history may be usefully considered in terms of three great cycles or periods, each of which began with a burst of creative activity permeating a sizable majority of our people. Each of these cycles began in response to the emergence of dynamic new economic and social problems for which the previous movement held no adequate answer.

Each called forth not only new concepts of governmental responsibility but new political orientation on the part of a great many citizens. Each accepted the economic and social changes which the earlier movement had produced in its period of creative energy, and moved on to develop new answers to the new challenge. Each was identified in its earlier dynamic stage with a leader of great stature, with Jefferson, with Lincoln, and with Franklin Roosevelt.

Each was launched in an atmosphere charged with surging enthusiasm and bitter partisanship, followed by a mellowing as the new concepts brought forth by the new conditions became more generally accepted and, ultimately, were adopted as basic objectives by both major political parties.

I believe that we are now in an advanced stage of the third of these political cycles, and that a new cycle, calling for new alignments and a fresh burst of political imagination and creative leadership, may now be in the early phases of its development.

Only a very brave or very foolish man would attempt, as this is written, to prophesy the outcome of the 1956 election. But if I am correct in the broad picture which I have just sketched, there are certain aspects of the approaching campaign which can be forecast with some confidence.

For instance, those questions which later historians will certainly judge to be the most crucial of our time will not be the principal subjects of debate. The campaign will be fought for the most part on older and more familiar ground.

As in past elections the Democrats will be denounced as radical New Dealers who favor an overbearing federal government and creeping socialism. Their proposals for a $1.25 minimum wage, increases in social security, farm price support programs, and expanded slum clearance will be described as starry-eyed Utopianisms, derived straight from Karl Marx. Their candidates will be labeled "soft on communism."

The Republicans will not get off much easier. It will be said that they are reactionary successors to Herbert Hoover who may lead us straight into another Great Depression. Proposals for a $1.00 minimum wage, more moderate increases in social security, lower price supports, and more limited public housing will be characterized as timid, reactionary, and dictated by Wall Street.

The Democrats, to defend themselves against the reproach of softness on communism, will be inclined to take a "tough" line on foreign policy issues; and the Republicans, in an effort to breathe more substance into the "peace" half of their "Peace and Prosperity" slogan, will call piously for a patient bipartisanship.

Few thoughtful Americans will be really happy about the narrow dimensions of this somewhat musty debate. Many leaders in both parties, members of the press, and ordinary citizens will sense in their hearts that these are clashes on the level of sloganeering, which do not reflect deeply felt rifts in national opinion. Yet of those who sense the vastly more significant questions which are taking shape offstage, few will be able to articulate them. And those who are will be warned by the professionals that these issues are too complicated for debate in an election year.

These prophecies are neither reckless nor novel. Most of us are aware that the heat generated by our recent national election campaigns arises largely from conflicts only remotely related to the great issues around which the history of the second half of the twentieth century will ultimately be written. We have become accustomed to this state of affairs, and only rarely do we bother to ask ourselves what can be done about it.

We may even remind each other that this is not a new thing. In 1928 the possibility of a world-wide depression of catastrophic proportions was not discussed. In the election of 1932, at the depth of the depression, Franklin Roosevelt preached economy and promised a balanced budget as the surest path to economic recovery.

❈   ❈   ❈

A CLOSER examination of the forces and habits of mind which have fashioned our political system may help to clarify some of the problems posed for both our political parties by the pressures of today's almost overwhelming world. Such an analysis may take as its starting point the words of James Madison in the tenth *Federalist* in 1787. "The most common and durable source of factions," he wrote, "has been the various and unequal distribution of property. Those who hold and those who are without property have ever formed distinct interests in society. Those who are creditors, and those who are debtors, fall under a like discrimination. A landed interest, a manufacturing interest, a mercantile interest, a monied interest, with many lesser interests, grow up of necessity in civilized nations, and divide them into different classes actuated by different sentiments and views."

In this shrewd paragraph, Madison foresaw much that was to remain with us throughout our political history. But one important factor he failed to foresee: that these interests, economically grounded for the most part, would not, as in many other democratic countries, conduct their quarrels through narrow, specialized political organizations. Instead, throughout most of our history, they would seek to further their interests by alliances created within the structures of two major political parties.

Americans are natural joiners, quick to create new organizations to combat whatever they feel may be wrong in their community or in their nation. Yet American political history is strewn with the wreckage of economic and social movements which attempted to become political parties in their own right.

The two dominant parties, which have survived these splinter efforts, have developed their own traditions and characteristic attitudes. But the very vastness of our country and the workings of our federal system have prevented them from achieving cohesiveness, discipline, or clear-cut ideologies. They have served instead as rather loosely defined arenas through which the pressures created by the interests that Madison described are filtered and compromised.

American political life, as I have suggested, can be seen in terms of a few relatively long periods, each dominated by a fairly stable coalition of these interests — a semipermanent majority with a rough consensus on immediate public questions. Each new coalition has found its instrument in one of the two major political parties. Which one has been determined by a complex interaction of traditions and loyalties, leadership and inspiration, strategy and accident. Because that party has been identified with a widely accepted view on current issues, it has developed a commanding position in the national government.

In the early phases of the cycle, when the new forces which created the new alignment are most dynamic and the public response most clear-cut, the electoral majorities of the dominant party may be overwhelming. Although long voting habits may keep many who share the new majority viewpoint within the fold of the opposition party, in the beginning that party is commonly the haven for those who reject the new consensus. The leaders of this group secure control of the party machinery and position it vigorously against the views widely accepted by the majority of citizens. This blindness to the new political realities consigns it to the role of semipermanent opposition.

Repeated defeat at the polls, however, leads to an intraparty struggle in an effort to bring the minority party position into closer harmony with what is by now clearly identified as the broad majority view. Meanwhile, as the majority party gains the policy objectives of the consensus it loses its momentum and the two parties grow closer together. In this way each ultimately comes to reflect, though with important differences of attitude and emphasis, the general position of the underlying consensus among the public at large.

In each of these long periods the minority party has been able, of course, to interrupt the rule of the majority party for short intervals. Indeed, as the questions raised by new forces began to shoulder aside those earlier ones which gave form and shape to the movement itself, the interruptions tended to become more frequent. As the movement matured it has lost its fervor, new personalities have often given the minority party temporary advantages; long years in office has led to a lethargy and lowering of standards in the party which was first to identify itself with the general consensus.

Yet a fundamental change in the direction of our government has always awaited the emergence of urgent and compelling new problems powerful enough to shatter the old majority-minority alignment. Around these new questions has emerged a new consensus, a brilliant new leadership, and a new semipermanent division of the voters into majority and minority groups. Each new alignment has been substantially altered from the one which preceded it, not only in its ideological reaction to the new challenge but also in its geographic and economic characteristics. Invariably the new division has been reflected in a shift in the nature, composition, or role of the two political parties.

Now let us see whether I can sketch our political history in terms of this general pattern.

This history, as I have suggested, may be divided into three periods of the type which I have described. The ideological nature of the consensus that dominated each of these cycles cannot easily be summed up in a paragraph, much less in a phrase. Each was complex, interwoven, and subject to constant changes in emphasis to meet current political pressures.

Yet at the risk of oversimplification it may be

said that the first, which extended from Jefferson's victory in 1800 to the outbreak of the Civil War in 1861, was characterized by a general acceptance, for the first time in history, of an effective federal government closely responsive to the majority will. In a sense it was a synthesis of two concepts which were presumed to be antagonistic: the federalism of Hamilton and the democratic faith of Jefferson and Jackson.

The second, which started in 1861 with Lincoln and ran until Franklin D. Roosevelt's election in 1932, imposed on this primary foundation a dynamic and uniquely American response to the Industrial Revolution. This involved an imaginative use of the corporate institution, the broadening of civil rights, and the expansion of economic opportunities through the settlement of the West and immigration from Europe.

The third, which encompasses the period from 1932 to the present day, reflects a general acceptance of governmental responsibility for minimum standards of living and opportunity and for the full use of our human and capital resources within a system of private ownership.

In the background, normally accepted by all but a fringe of extremists, has been a still broader area of agreement on the ground rules under which the political struggle is to be conducted. These ground rules assume the validity of the democratic process and the denial of the right of the majority unreasonably to impose its will on the minority. On the one occasion when the minority opposing the general consensus in both parties attempted to change these ground rules, the result was civil war.

*　　*　　*

Lᴇᴛ us examine now the general characteristics of the majority consensus and its opposition in the first of the three periods, as they have been reflected in the political parties. Any brief sketch that I make here must, of course, be subject to qualifications and amendments of details, as is the case with all such generalizations. I may add that this first period in particular is also subject to varied historic interpretations, which are vigorously maintained and persuasively presented by opposing schools of thought.

However, the broad picture, with a few exceptions, notably the later Jackson period, shows the South and West aligned against the Northeastern Seaboard minority. The West at that time, of course, covered principally the area between the Alleghanies and the Mississippi and from Kentucky and Tennessee northward. Towards the end, it began to embrace the area now included in the tier of states just west of the Mississippi.

Whether this alignment reflected sectional interests rather than economic interests remains a point of difference among historians, which leads me to believe that it reflected some of both. Economic interests were to some extent at least sectional. The new West was a frontier — rough, brawling, individualistic, and continually in debt. Although the South was more stable, it was also an agricultural region, putting more and more new land to the plow, and burdened with the institution of slavery. Their common debtor status generally bound these two regions together against the merchant and manufacturing Eastern Seaboard, and the ties of trade moving down the broad Ohio and Mississippi sealed the bond.

But circumstance and environment played their shaping part. The man of the new West hacked his farm from the forest with his own hands, defended himself as best he could, and educated his children before his own fireside or in rude schools. He could have used the beneficent intervention of a strong government in Washington, and often sought it vigorously by way of such "internal improvements" as roads and canals and free or cheap land. But difficulties of communication prevented him from placing too much reliance upon remote governmental support against the immediate hazards of the frontier.

Thus the Westerner developed a strong individualist strain. He accepted the federal government as a permanent and necessary fixture. Yet his principal desire was to be let alone to make his own way. These political notions fell in easily with those of the Southern planter, who mixed a manorial way of life with an English liberal tradition.

By contrast, the Eastern business interest in sound money and the encouragement of budding factories looked to a stronger central government, but even more important, to a government manned by "sound" conservatives. This ideological division is classically personified in the conflict between Jefferson and Hamilton.

The majority consensus, which developed out of these pressures and conflicts, supported the development of a federal government adequate to its growing responsibilities, but insisted that it be firmly rooted in democratic principles. Its political instrument was the Republican party, later to change its name to Democratic. In 1800 it was swept into power with Jefferson by a smashing popular majority.

Despite the bitter opposition he had faced from the conservative-minded Federalists, Jefferson sensed the wide scope of the underlying agreement that brought about his victory. "We are all Republicans, we are all Federalists," he said in his inaugural. But it took Monroe and an "era of good feeling" to make the point for the country and even for historians.

Tradition has it that this era was unique in our history, and so it was if we focus only upon the absence of a formally organized political party in opposition to the party in power. If we consider, however, both the character of the questions that engaged the efforts of the national government and the nature of the consensus that supported the successive administrations, we find a situation which is not unique at all. In fact, it may be said without too much distortion that eras of good feelings are almost chronic in our political history. We are living in one right now.

The tenure of Jefferson's followers in Washington was broken by the victory of John Quincy Adams in 1824. Though formally a "Jeffersonian," as were almost all politicians of the era of good feeling, it is generally agreed that Adams was not in the main stream of popular Jefferson-Jackson democracy. The triumph of the forces which he represented was short-lived, but it requires some attention because it is characteristic of these interruptions.

Adams' victory was made possible only by a split in the ranks of the coalition which made up the majority consensus. Many of Andrew Jackson's frontier supporters were thought to be too assertive and too insistent on their unaided strength. Other groups in the majority broke away because of local pressures. Although Jackson won a plurality of the popular vote, the three-cornered election was thrown into the House of Representatives, where political maneuver concurred with defections from Jackson led by Henry Clay, and gave Adams the election.

Thus significant fissures in the majority were exposed. They were to be subjected to continuous pressures by new problems, as yet barely perceived, until in 1860 the whole existing political structure collapsed, and was replaced by a new majority-minority division along substantially different lines of interest. We shall see similar forces at work in each of the remaining two cycles of broadly accepted political consensus.

By 1824, however, the momentum of the first majority coalition was by no means exhausted nor were the widely supported claims and interests represented by the Democratic party yet fully established. With the election of 1828 came the vigorous reassertion of the rights of the common man, both urban and rural, in the tumultuous triumph of Jacksonian democracy, for which Jefferson's victory a quarter-century before had laid the groundwork.

There followed, in turn, the rapid extension of adult manhood suffrage throughout the Union, the spread of free public education, and the melodrama of Jackson's conflict with the Second Bank of the United States — a conflict by which he symbolized the clash between the newly enfranchised voters of the frontier and of the eastern industrialized centers, on the one hand, and the conservative financial interests of the older parts of the country, on the other.

Although these were times of notable achievement, they mark the final burst of creative energy of the first majority coalition. Democrats continued after Jackson to be elected with reasonable frequency. Yet, if we put aside their pursuit of manifest destiny in Texas and the West, the Democrats had no novel programs or policies to propose which were particularly geared to the unfilled domestic needs of the party's majority constituency, and periods of Whig tenure became more common.

A last flicker of the old creative energy is seen in the first Homestead Act, introduced by Senator Andrew Johnson in 1846. Yet, on the whole, these changes in party control of the government did not bring about changes related to differences of party outlook, in broad governmental policies, or in the lives of ordinary people.

The diminishing influence of the Jefferson-Jackson majority was accelerated by the Whig skill in stealing not only their issues but their democratic techniques. As early as 1802, Hamilton, seeing the success of Jefferson's direct, popular appeal to the voters, recognized the Whig need for more effective electioneering techniques. Thirty-eight years later, Hamilton's political descendents in the "log cabin and hard cider elections" of 1840 embarked on a political campaign which marked in one sense a turning point in our political history.

A well-intentioned military man of limited talents, General William Henry Harrison, opposed Martin Van Buren and beat the Democrats at their own game. The well-financed Whig nominee campaigned as the poor man's candidate, born in a log cabin, simple, honest, dedicated to the people's interest. Martin Van Buren, Democratic successor to Andrew Jackson, the hero of the common man, was depicted as an aristocrat who lived on champagne, ate off gold plates, scented his whiskers with French perfume, and wore corsets.

With the help of such slogans as "Harrison, two dollars a day and roast beef," the general won easily, thereby illustrating the fact that when the issues in politics have become hazy, personalities, money, and techniques count double. The symbolism of representing the common man had been recognized as crucial. The first consensus had won its day.

The Democrats regained their control of the government under Polk and a program of Western expansion, only to lose it to his victorious general, Zachary Taylor, whose views on public questions were disturbing to almost no one.

As the energy and cohesiveness of the Democratic majority dwindled, the issue which was finally to shatter the old political alignment came with in-

creasing intensity to the fore. In the early years of
the nineteenth century, it was clear to many thoughtful people, Jefferson among them, that the institution of slavery posed questions that America as a
nation could not avoid forever.

The 1840's and 1850's saw these questions moving
into the areas of public debate, while the resources
of compromise within the existing political framework were tried and exhausted. It became increasingly apparent that this framework was inadequate
to the basic issue, because the interests involved
were different and indeed cut across the party lines
marked out by the existing framework.

Moreover, the tensions within the dominant political majority, focused most sharply by the slavery
question, were reinforced by other developments at
work in the country. With the coming, first, of the
canals and, later and more powerfully, of the east-
west railroads, the axis of trade with the West and
the frontier shifted from a north-south line along
the Mississippi River to an east-west line from the
interior to the Atlantic Seaboard.

This reorientation frayed the political bonds which
had generally held together the West and the
South. As the old "West" turned into the "Mid-
west," it became more stable and settled. Industry
began to follow agriculture over the mountains.

The South, depending upon extensive cotton ex-
ports to England, had everything to gain by trade in

a free international market. The industrial centers, old and new, wanted protection from foreign competition. And the Western farmers, with their markets not abroad but in the Eastern manufacturing sections, were content with higher tariffs as well. Concessions to ease Southern antagonism by focusing the tariff structure more on revenue and less on protection failed to convince the South that the North was not determined to hold it in economic bondage.

These questions were submitted to the ultimate resolution of war. And we have come to regard them as the one complex of problems in our history which eluded solution within our constitutional framework. Of course, this is so; but to the extent that this minimizes the elements of political readjustment and realignment which entered into the solution, it is a false picture.

These elements added up to a shift in the semi-permanent majority coalition, and the emergence in 1854 of a new political instrument, the Republican party. Bearing the name of Jefferson's party, which had fallen into disuse, it made its first appearance in Jackson, Michigan, and six years later elected its first president.

❈   ❈   ❈

T HE first two successful national tickets of that party illustrate the nature and makeup of the new majority: Lincoln, a Western frontiersman by birth and an old Whig in politics, acquainted through his law practice with the new ties binding the West to the East; Hannibal Hamlin of Maine, Lincoln's first vice-president, from the old stronghold of Federalism on the Eastern Seaboard; Andrew Johnson, Lincoln's second running mate, an old Jacksonian Democrat, symbolizing the frontier element in Jacksonian democracy.

The decade of the American Civil War saw great changes in Europe and the mergence of Canada as a dominion. But nowhere were these years as fateful as in the United States.

The war decided primarily that the nation would not be split in two. In the process of so deciding it called forth a surge of energy, physical and moral alike, almost without parallel in history. Huge armies were raised, equipped, and maintained in the field; the industrial revolution was greatly speeded up; and as Lincoln suggested at Gettysburg, democratic government gave the world an extraordinary demonstration of its vigor and moral capacity. The American nation passed through the test of fire and emerged with a new strength and purpose scarcely conceived before 1860.

The Republican party, as the party of victory and unity, was faced with a unique opportunity, and by political techniques both legitimate and otherwise it proceeded to take full advantage of it.

An alliance was promptly made with the new fast-developing forces of industry. To this powerful interest was added the pensioners of the Grand Army of the Republic, the farmers of the new states of the Middle West, the recently enfranchised Negroes, and many newly made citizen-immigrants of the industrial North and East.

This new consensus continued to dominate American politics for seventy years, until the shock of the Great Depression of 1929–1933 brought about new alignments. The Republican party, as its chosen instrument, governed during most of this period, interrupted only by brief Democratic interludes. Yet between Grant and McKinley the Republican grip remained tenuous. Plagued with corruption and the arrogant behavior of many of its leaders, it maintained itself in power only by disenfranchising much of the South and by gerrymandering without conscience.

In 1884, even these expedients failed, and Cleveland was elected for two nonconsecutive terms. However, by 1896 the Republican party had not only washed away much of the bad taste of its postwar behavior, but, even more important, had succeeded in identifying itself completely with the interests of the dominant consensus. The result was the landslide election of McKinley, which was reminiscent of Jackson's victories, especially that of 1832.

It will be worthwhile to pause for a moment to examine the Cleveland interlude. Even more clearly than that of Adams' sixty years earlier, it was made possible by the temporary defection of one segment of the still dominant majority. In this case it was the "Mugwumps," the more radical, reforming wing of the Republican party. This defection, like its earlier counterpart, revealed a weakness in the new coalition which many years later was to prove its undoing.

Yet the policies which Cleveland followed in his two alternate terms, produced little by way of basic divergence from the policies of his Republican predecessors. This reflected the power of the consensus. We remember them for the passage of the Civil Service Act and the Interstate Commerce Act. The latter, of course, contained ideas capable of far-reaching development. At the time, however, it was conceived as a relatively mild reform.

Cleveland's Republican successors permit us to follow in detail the development of the forces which had brought about the split revealed by Cleveland's victory. One portion of the majority party insisted upon the highest purity of the laissez-faire concepts on which the Republicans had ridden to power; the other struggled to break with its past inertia and to cope with new problems, as yet only vaguely felt and largely misunderstood.

The debunking propensity, which seems to be an occupational delight among many professional historians, has divested the administrations of Theodore Roosevelt of some of the glamor which, as Dean Acheson vividly recalls, they had for the men who lived through them. Yet even if we rate those years high in creativity, it cannot be denied that they reveal, like Jackson's administrations, the early signs of a political autumn.

Moreover, Theodore Roosevelt was not able to stamp his impress permanently upon his party. The traditional concepts on which it had been based were too deep and too powerful for that. The revolt of the Bull Moose against the traditionalists, which split the Republican party, followed in 1912, and with it the disintegration of this, the second semipermanent majority in our history, began in earnest.

Yet political alignments are far more durable than they appear to be. Although the defection provided the immediate occasion for Wilson's two terms, it did not yet mark the end of the Republican domination. Heavily influenced by big business, many Republican leaders were growing indifferent to the real interests of their farmer-Negro-immigrant constituency, which had carried their party so far. Yet as in the post-Jacksonian era, the old momentum of habit and loyalty awaited an even sterner shock.

Behind the confusion caused by the developing war, that shock, destined ultimately to blow the old political alignments sky-high, was in the making. And to understand how it came about, we must, once more with an expansive generality for which I hope I may be forgiven, examine more closely the important economic and social trends which marked the period of Republican dominance.

The movement that dominated this long era was the economic growth of America. This involved the development of the nation's transportation and communication networks, the construction of its basic industrial capacity, the extension of the area of settlement clear to the West Coast, and the filling of the country with people.

Although this work of economic development began from a higher base, it was similar in many ways to what we now see being undertaken in much of Asia, Africa, and South America, where the social structure is beginning to feel the full impact of the industrial revolution which we faced a century ago.

Some Republicans in our day dislike being reminded of how massively government beneficence contributed to this development. The tariff provided genuine protection to new industries as yet unable to withstand the competition of their more mature counterparts abroad. Vast acreage of the public domain given free to the railroads provided a major subsidy for transportation development. Some historians assert that these grants, the total extent of which exceeded that of the entire state of Texas, were sufficient to pay for all railroad construction of this period. The continuation of the homestead free-land policy further encouraged the rapid occupation and exploitation of the remaining public lands.

Meanwhile, markets for domestic consumption expanded with every boatload of immigrants from Europe. As our booming economy cried for new capital, the high profits were reinvested to earn more and still more. At the turn of the century, the United States economic growth was already outstripping that of any other country.

The consensus of this long period accepted *laissez faire* as a one-way street which assumed the propriety of massive governmental subsidies while it forbade public regulation or control of the new industrial resources. So conceived, it was enforced not only by public opinion but by the courts as well, on those occasions when public opinion momentarily forgot its task. State and federal laws requiring the new industry to pay a larger share of the social costs of its growth were consistently declared unconstitutional.

Although our tradition now emphasizes the magnitude of these social costs, we do this period an injustice when we characterize it as the age of "robber barons" and the "age of reaction." On the contrary, it involved an enormous organization of effort and energy, accomplished largely, though not exclusively, through private means. Moreover, in its essence it was one of the most exhilarating eras of innovation in our history.

Human and social costs were certainly heavy. Yet no comparable economic growth has ever been without them. As we look at the five-year plans of foreign governments, democratic and totalitarian alike, we can predict with some confidence that there will be no modern exceptions to this rule.

In America, at least, the sharp edge of economic pressure was blunted by our peculiar advantages. As long as there was free land for the asking in the West, no workman, however poor, was hopelessly trapped in a city slum. No doubt it took a good deal of energy and initiative to break free. But the alternative was a real one and vivid to the imagination.

Traditional attitudes and patterns of social mobility, rooted in the earlier Democratic era, were thus reinforced in this period of Republican economic development. Thus firmly ingrained, they have contributed immensely to the creation of an open American society which belies the conceptual analysis of Karl Marx.

Following the Civil War, the Republicans, as the

dominant, victorious political party facing the divided and demoralized Democrats, became identified by the complex process of interaction earlier described with this broadly supported program of economic development. This enabled them quickly to capture its leadership. Republican political platforms clearly and confidently expressed this identification: *laissez faire,* high tariffs, free land in the West, subsidies for our railroads, and unlimited immigration from overseas to fill up the country and provide cheap factory labor.

During this period the Democrats, as is typical of the semipermanent opposition party, were left by default with nothing to do but agree on general principles and oppose on specific details. For years it remained the party of "me tooism," dedicated to the task of proving its respectability.

The opposition of the more liberal Democratic wing took the form of sharp and sometimes effective criticism of the excesses of the Republican majority, together with support for economic and social reform. In election years these Democrats, without opposing the laissez-faire philosophy directly, pointed to human wreckage lying in the wake of the expanding economic and financial juggernaut — the child labor, the slums, the factories without proper fire protection or safety devices, the recurrent bank panics and depressions.

Wilson's "New Freedom" programs in 1912 reflected these traditional Democratic concerns until the war forced him to abandon his domestic efforts. Yet like Cleveland he did not challenge directly the broadly accepted views on which the Republicans had based their long tenure in office. The principal elements in his program were the monetary reform of the Federal Reserve Act, the enactment of an income tax law, and the strengthening of the antitrust laws — concepts easily reconcilable with the generally accepted economic premises which underlay the period of Republican dominance.

The Federal Reserve System was a new approach to the sound money objective, which avoided, it was thought, the evils of a central bank. The income tax was made possible by a constitutional amendment adopted under a Republican administration. And the Sherman Act, whose objectives Wilson further sought to attain by the Clayton Act, bears the name of a Republican senator and was enacted by a Republican Congress.

The new antitrust laws, in fact, provide one of the clearest illustrations of the reformist character of the Wilson program. They were not conceived as regulatory devices, but rather as a means for attacking unusual situations which prevented industry itself from being self-regulating, and, more important for Wilson, as a means of giving the little man a chance to start a business himself. Once normal conditions were restored, it was assumed, both the

economic objective of efficiency and the social objective of independent enterprise would again be
assured by the unchecked operation of the competi-
tive process.

This contrasts sharply with our modern conception of the antitrust laws as essentially regulatory
measures which operate for consciously stated public ends, and our growing awareness that in some
fields, at least, efficiency and independence may
not be handmaidens but opponents.

As long as the country was caught in the exciting
sweep of a continuing extensive economic development, the appeal of Democratic critics, for a better
balance between material gain and social justice,
made little impact either upon the dominant majority view or upon any substantial segment of that
majority. In an important way this illustrates the
traditional plight of the opposition in our political
system: in the absence of a really *fundamental*
change in conditions, it is unable to substitute its
views for the views of a clearly established majority. It can only accept the broadly supported consensus of what needs to be done and promise to do
it better, cheaper, quicker, or with greater integrity
than the party which achieved dominance by first
identifying itself with these objectives.

In the nature of things, however, the extensive
economic development of the latter half of the
nineteenth century could not continue forever to

provide a basis for a majority political consensus. Already, in the closing years of that century, signs began to appear that this growth was losing its dynamism.

The first inroads upon the policy of free and unlimited immigration resulted from the Chinese Exclusion Act of 1882. Strains began to appear in the relationship that bound the financial and industrial East to the agricultural West, strains which were reflected in the sporadic political upthrust of agrarian discontent under Populist leadership.

Once the free land in the West began to be exhausted, it became clear that the relationship was not so mutually advantageous as it had first seemed. And the closing of the frontier marked a change of enormous consequence.

These developments were in some ways obscured and further complicated by the First World War and the emergence of the United States as a world power and a creditor nation. But they continued to work inexorably, and by the 1920's they had reached an acute stage.

It may be said that the crash of 1929 and the subsequent depression were inevitable because we did not know how to shift from *extensive* economic development, based on the filling up of our country and unrestrained exploitation of its resources, to *intensive* economic development, based on the rapid, systematic expansion of purchasing power in depth.

Indeed, neither the people nor political leaders in either party foresaw in time the need for such a shift.

The early postwar 1920's were studded by a series of bitter and violent industrial strikes. But the unions, blocked by hostile legal decisions, and with many of their members drifting away, lacked the economic power necessary to force a broader distribution of the fruits of production. Within limits, employers continued to decide what slice of the sales dollar went to wages. In most instances they chose to keep the slice as small as possible.

The economic result was both interesting and explosive. Between 1923 and 1929 the technology of manufacturing was changing rapidly, and factory output per man hour rose 24 per cent. With wages moving up only 3 per cent, wage *costs* were materially reduced, while prices remained stable.

This meant that profits climbed sharply. But climbing was not enough; they had to have some place to go from there. With a relatively low level of taxation, they flowed first into creating new production facilities. When it became apparent that the relatively stabilized purchasing power could not support these expanding facilities, profits were diverted into massive private loans abroad, most of which could not be repaid, and finally into a wild securities speculation.

Meanwhile, tariff policies which may have been

sensible for a young debtor nation trying to expand
its own productive plant were pushed to new ex-
tremes, at a time when the underlying economic
situation had changed completely. The war and its
aftermath had turned us into the creditor, and if
other nations were to be able to pay us what they
owed, they had to be able to sell us their goods.
Moreover, our own expanding industrial capacity
needed the external markets which only expanded
foreign trade could provide. In the 1920's, in the
face of these requirements, United States tariffs
were not reduced but rather raised to the dizziest
heights in history.

In retrospect, one of the most remarkable features
about this development is that no prominent econo-
mist except R. G. Tugwell and no publication except
the financial page of the *New York Times*, as far as
I know, foresaw the disaster that lay just over the
hill.

✽   ✽   ✽

IN the campaign of 1932 Franklin
Roosevelt called for a wider range of measures to
deal with the growing crisis, which, he said, must
be attacked like an enemy in war. Yet the views
which had shaped and maintained the old consensus
were not quickly discarded even by the supposedly

"radical" father of the New Deal. On October 19, only three weeks before the election, he told his listeners:

I regard reduction in Federal spending as one of the most important issues of this campaign. In my opinion, it is the most direct and effective contribution the Government can make to business.

This statement came towards the end of a speech on the federal budget, in which he offered the following traditional analysis of our difficulties:

On the plain question of frugality of management . . . we find that the expenditure for the business of government in 1927 was $2,187,000,000 and in 1931, $3,168,-000,000.

This increase . . . is the most reckless and extravagant that I have been able to discover in the statistical record of any peacetime government, anywhere, anytime.

Mr. Roosevelt then went even further in support of the outmoded economic concepts which the majority had supported for three generations.

The Republican administration is committed to the idea that we ought to center control of everything in Washington as rapidly as possible — federal control . . .

I shall approach the problem by carrying out the plain concept of our Party, which is to reduce the cost of Federal Government operations by 25 per cent.

Of course that means a complete realignment of the unprecedented bureaucracy that has assembled in Washington in the past four years.

It is obviously unfair to characterize Mr. Roosevelt's 1932 campaign by excerpts from this one speech — for on many other occasions in that difficult year he presented a far more positive philosophy of governmental responsibility. Yet it is interesting and instructive to compare these particular words with those of Abraham Lincoln in his First Inaugural in 1861:

Apprehension seems to exist among the people of the Southern states that by the accession of a Republican administration their property and their peace and personal security are to be endangered. There has never been any reasonable cause for such apprehension. Indeed, the most ample evidence to the contrary . . . is found in nearly all the published speeches of him who now addresses you.

I do but quote from one of those speeches when I declare that "I have no purpose, directly or indirectly, to interfere with the institution of slavery where it exists. I believe I have no lawful right to do so, and I have no inclination to do so." Those who nominated and elected me did so with full knowledge that I had made this and many similar declarations, and had never recanted them.

Lincoln and Roosevelt were men of rare insight and courage. But each, as he stood on the brink of his new age, found it difficult to break with the familiar language and concepts of an earlier day. With the limited perspective of their times the full dimensions of the upheaval which lay ahead were but dimly seen.

Today we are certainly no better prepared to foresee the nature of the profound changes which may confront us in the next decade, and as the pressures increase we shall find it no easier to abandon outworn slogans and habits of thinking. We may only hope that as the new challenge takes shape, leaders will emerge whose capacity for understanding and action equals that of their great predecessors. We shall, I believe, need them badly.

But let us return to our chronicle. By 1933 the extent of the economic debacle could scarcely be denied. Like the new issues of the 1860's, the new problem of restoring the health of our economy and changing the direction of its future development to avert similar catastrophies cut across the old majority-minority lines. They could hardly be treated within the existing party framework because neither party at that time was geared to the new requirements. The Republican party was committed by its history and its view of its constituency to a policy of unrestrained individualism, while the Democrats were committed to a reformist quest for a greater measure of social justice within the old economic concepts.

Thus the crash and subsequent depression shattered the old majority coalition, which had survived for nearly eighty years, and replaced it with what has

proved to be the third semipermanent political alignment in our history. The relative absence this time
of clear geographical factors was a reflection of improved techniques in communication and transportation, although some opposition areas did develop
in the Northeast and within the farm belt.

Most Americans, however, threw their support
behind a totally new approach to the problem of
economic security — an approach dramatically opposed to the majority concepts which both parties
had supported for generations. The principal line
of demarcation between the new majority and its
opponents was drawn between the "haves" and the
"have-nots," and perhaps more sharply drawn than
in any period since Jackson's. Farmers, Negroes, and
the sons and daughters of the foreign-born were
shaken loose from their traditional political moorings.

In ideological terms, the new majority supported
increased intervention by the central government in
the economic life of the nation, while the minority
clung stubbornly and nostalgically to variations of
laissez faire.

The Democrats were in the best position politically and the best prepared philosophically to identify themselves with the new attitudes. In Franklin
Roosevelt they had a brilliant leader of great popular appeal, who was able quickly to identify himself
with the hopes and fears of workers, farmers, and
small businessmen.

Yet old habits change slowly in politics, as elsewhere, and the promise of an expanding, full-production economy was not immediately grasped. For some time the leaders of the Democratic New Deal continued to conceive of themselves as carrying out their older platform of reform. They looked on hunger in the midst of plenty, the squalor of the slums, the insecurity of old age, the power advantages of the corporations in dealing with labor, the economic difficulties of our farmers; and they judged them as injustices which must be rectified.

Although full employment was accepted as an ultimate goal, there were many ready to assume that it might never be achieved except in occasional boom periods. Moreover, the laissez-faire consensus of predepression days still exerted a lingering influence. Even after its resounding victory in 1936, the Democratic administration failed to press ahead in its effort to increase purchasing power, expand production, and eliminate mass unemployment. It chose instead to place its primary emphasis on a balanced budget. The result was the sharp recession of 1937.

Some government economists agreed with those business leaders who believed that we had reached an economic plateau on which six or eight million chronically unemployed would be an unfortunate but inevitable byproduct. The government's primary responsibility, as they saw it, was to try to keep economic and social injustices at a minimum within the presumably fixed boundaries of the so-called "mature economy."

The social and political implications of this "mature economy" concept were as dangerous as they were novel, in a nation with a traditional passion for expansion. Those who assumed that the production pie was unlikely to grow substantially larger reasoned that no economic group could get ahead except by taking something from some other group.

Thus many businessmen came to believe that they could increase their profits only by keeping wages down and putting prices up. Many union leaders were convinced that their members could only improve their living standards by squeezing wage increases out of profits. Many farmers came to regard both groups not as potential customers but as natural economic adversaries.

It is safe to say, however, that the "mature economy" theory was never more than a rationalization developed in an attempt to appease a demand that no one quite knew how to satisfy within our existing economic and political framework. Yet a scarcity economy, in which group was inevitably set against group and in which injustices were mitigated but opportunities remained limited, was only half a loaf. The evolving public conceptions of the Welfare State, for in essence the consensus of the 1930's was an agreement on the welfare state, inevitably came to

include, as an essential objective, "full employment."
It is in fact this concept of an expanding economy,
fully employing its resources of men, machines, and
capital, which gives the American concept of the
welfare state its distinctive character.

When the war revealed the enormous productive
potential of our economic system, this demand for
full employment began to grow more articulate. Yet
as late as 1946, when, as Director of Economic
Stabilization, I suggested a gross national product of
$200 billion with 60 million people at work by 1948
as an attainable economic objective, I was promptly
labeled a visionary.

The people in the streets, however, were asking
tough questions which reflected their broader concept of the new consensus. If the American productive machine can keep all of us employed for destruc-
tive purposes in time of war, they wondered, why
can't it provide constructive jobs for all of us in
times of peace?

The Republicans, heavily laden with the traditions
of their golden age, after a brief period of panicky
cooperation with the New Deal had subsided into
the usual opposition role of the party which repre-
sents the nonassenting minority. They had fulfilled
this classic role by soundly damning the New Deal
and all its works, at a pitch which reached its peak
of intensity in the immediate prewar years.

In 1946, the Republican party was able to capitalize on the frustrations and impatience of the immediate postwar period to gain a short-lived control of the Congress. By 1948, however, the American people had ceased to fear plenty, and the Democrats, who were first to catch the vision of full employment through intensive economic development in time of peace, were able thereby to strengthen their identification with the new consensus and to recapture control of the government.

One sees in the defection of the South and some other regular Democratic areas in the elections of 1948 and 1952 the kind of split which made possible the victory of opposition presidential candidates in 1824 and 1884. And we see in the close congressional results in 1952 and in the Democratic recovery of control of Congress in 1954 indications that the majority remains relatively intact and reluctant to desert its traditional political instrument. But we should not confuse these signs of persisting strength with those of youthful political vigor.

The critical period of the New Deal constituted no less than a revolution in American life, and most Americans look back on it now as a time of hope and high national purpose. In spite of attacks no less vicious than those launched at Andrew Jackson a century earlier, Franklin Roosevelt has held his extraordinary place in the hearts of a majority of the American people.

Roosevelt's principal domestic political achievement was the forging of a new coalition of farmers, workers, small businessmen, and intellectuals, who had become aware of the inadequacy of old answers to new problems and who welcomed his leadership. The crisis which he faced in 1933 was as basic as that which Lincoln faced in 1861, and in a sense his response was no less important to the future health and security of the Republic.

＊   ＊   ＊

ONE further point must be made before we conclude this admittedly sketchy historical survey. The three majority-minority alignments which I have outlined have been considered almost entirely from the standpoint of domestic issues, without regard for their impact on foreign affairs.

This does not mean that international pressures have not played their role in the development of our political structure. On the contrary, foreign affairs have absorbed the attention of our ablest leaders from the very beginnings of the republic. Of our first six presidents, four had previously served their country as Secretary of State.

The revolutionary fires which lighted Europe in the last years of the eighteenth century were reflected here in the struggle between "radicals" of

Jefferson and the "monarchists" of Hamilton. Their Napoleonic aftermath related itself to America in the Louisiana Purchase, the War of 1812, and the acquisition of Florida.

The fathers of the American Revolution themselves deliberately intended their own revolution to become a beacon fire to arouse subject peoples throughout the world. "I always consider the settlement of America with wonder and reverence," said John Adams, "as the opening for the emancipation of the slavish part of mankind all over the earth."

British and American objectives in the New World were merged to some extent in the Monroe Doctrine. Yet as manifest destiny pressed westward it was thrown into conflict with Britain, France, Mexico, Canada, Spain, and Russia. Perhaps the most significant legacy of this period in the field of foreign affairs was a kind of two-sided "keep out" sign: Americans, keep out of entangling alliances; and foreigners, keep out of the Americas.

In the second period, particularly the latter half, the impact of world affairs was more widespread in one sense but still, I judge, relatively incidental, except for the years of actual hostilities in World War I. Although the war with Spain and its unexpected colonial aftermath are worth special study in the light of present-day problems, at the time we took them in our stride. The debates between Senators Hoar and Beveridge on America's new imperialist role were between two leaders of the Republican majority. Bryan's effort to turn this issue to the advantage of the opposition proved unsuccessful.

We entered World War I despite the unanimous view of the political leaders of both parties in the election campaign only six months earlier that we could and should keep out. And Wilson's brave attempt to involve us permanently and constructively in the adjustment of international problems through the League of Nations ended in failure.

The third period shows a proportionate broadening of our international consensus, which we shall subsequently discuss in some detail. In this period, as Franklin Roosevelt and his successors came face to face with global problems, the groundwork laid by Woodrow Wilson a generation or more earlier proved invaluable. When he tackled the problems of international organization in the later years of the war, Mr. Roosevelt was on familiar ground. As the Democratic candidate for vice-president in the 1920 election, the principal burden in the fight for the League of Nations had rested on his shoulders.

Yet even the breadth and sweep of our current involvement in world affairs has not substantially shifted the focus of our political activity from its preoccupation with domestic problems. All this is implied in the old saw that partisan politics stops at the water's edge. Of course, it does not and never has. The dominant and opposition parties have gen-

erally taken more or less opposing sides on foreign
policy questions.

There has been this difference, however. Thus far,
at least, these matters have not entered integrally
into the broad public consensus, but have been introduced in a rather artificial way as secondary
issues. The party in power, when foreign questions
came to a head, has had to deal with them — has
had to *make* foreign policy. This is both a constitutional responsibility and a practical necessity. Those
who were already identified with that party on
domestic issues tended to accept and defend its
foreign policy position.

The late 1930's, in any event, were a time in which
a growing crisis abroad posed problems which no
responsible American administration could avoid.
The inevitable reinvolvement of this country with
European and world affairs thus created new differences, which were superimposed on the conflict
over domestic economic policy between the Democrats, representing the new consensus, and the Republican leaders, who still insisted that the New
Deal was an unfortunate but passing phase which,
given time, would ultimately blow over.

This theory of our political development has, of
course, vastly oversimplified a complex and inter-
acting process. But I am convinced that it contains
some important and neglected truths.

II

The New Deal Becomes Respectable

BY the outbreak of World War
II, a large majority of the American people had
reached far closer agreement on questions deeply
affecting the public interest than their leaders real-
ized. Moreover, this consensus or agreement was
not a result of the accompanying political debate,
which indeed tended to conceal it. Nor could it be
viewed as a painfully worked out compromise between two relatively equal antagonists holding opposing views.

The consensus, which in general supported the
Welfare State, had spread across the membership of
both political parties. In each party it was opposed
by minorities which clung to older concepts of government and economics. In the Democratic party,
which had maintained itself in power after winning

in 1932 by providing vigorous leadership for the
new consensus and asserting the policy positions
essential to its objectives, the minority was largely
confined to certain sections of the South. Here it was
vocal and strong, but beyond the area of civil rights,
in which seniority gave it a position of great strength
in the Senate, it was ineffective nationally.

The anticonsensus minority in the Republican
party, however, was able to play a more effective
national role. Although Republican candidates for
President, recognizing the general popular support
for New Deal measures, vigorously denied any desire to turn back the clock, the old guard was strong
enough heavily to color the positions and pronounce-
ments of their party. As a result, the existence of a
general agreement on the essentials of public policy
in the prewar years was not apparent in the official
party positions. On the contrary, in the late 1930's
and the early 1940's, just before our entry into
World War II, the political arena bristled with
sharply contested divisions between the leadership
of the two parties along the entire range of policies,
domestic and foreign.

So close was the congressional division on foreign
affairs that a whole series of critical measures leading up to our entry into World War II prevailed by
a majority of twenty votes or less in the lower house.
In the case of the extension of the "peacetime"
draft, three months before Pearl Harbor, the ma-

jority margin in the House of Representatives was a single vote. Even today, the cries of indignation and alarm which may be heard constantly on both sides of the political fence seem to contradict any assumption of popular agreement.

Yet these boilings and eruptions on the surface of our political life should not mislead us about the views of the rank and file of both parties and of the general electorate on what should be done and how we should go about it. Although the feuding and the fighting have both their function and their useful consequences, they obscure, as often as they illuminate, the real character of the political alignment in the country at large. For insight into this political development, we must look to what the parties actually *do* — the means and measures they support when vested with the responsibility of office — not merely to the words which they use to chastise each other on the hustings.

If, as I have maintained, a broad underlying public agreement on major issues started to develop in the early 1930's, under pressure of new forces, and was full-blown a decade later, why is it that this agreement has not been more clearly reflected in the behavior of the political parties?

To begin to answer this question, it may be useful to examine in more detail the wide scope of disagreement which exists, not only between the majority in each party which reflects the consensus and the minority in each party that opposes it, but within the ranks of those who make up these divisions. These differences are further intensified and distorted by election year conflicts, which often call forth the fierce expression of party loyalty and prejudice.

There is, for instance, ample room for wide differences within the consensus in intensity of support for particular programs. There is also room for differences about the measures best suited to carry out the broad purposes on which the majority has agreed. A consensus which encompasses the objective of full employment can legitimately include those who would place primary emphasis on the encouragement of capital formation, as well as those who favor measures designed to increase consumer purchasing power as means to the same end. The Democrats may vigorously reflect one view; the Republicans, the other.

A national consensus, then, as I see it, is no more or no less than a rough working agreement on major propositions of policy. Its bounds define, in effect, the area within which a compromise reached according to regularized procedures will be acceptable. This means, generally, that the details of the compromise are left to be worked out on the formal political level, or even below it, by the institutions, groups, and individuals most intimately affected by the particular method chosen.

As long as the compromise thus devised falls within the area marked out by the broad consensus, it will receive general support. Perhaps support is too strong a term to use in this connection, for it suggests an active element which is not necessarily present. Acquiescence, on the other hand, is too passive to convey my meaning. The quality of popular approval underlying these compromises which implement the rough working agreement lies between these poles. Consent may be the best word to describe it.

If this is true, it follows that once a new consensus has been reached in response to new problems, and once the initial period of political conflict between those leaders who recognize its significance and support it, and those who oppose it, has evolved into a period of general acceptance of the consensus by both parties, the principal function of the political parties and the formal political processes becomes clearly defined: the development of responsible means and measures for putting the consensus into effect in a manner which encroaches as little as possible upon the legitimate countervailing interests of the individuals and groups that may be adversely affected.

Consequently, as I have suggested, the role of the opposition party in each of the three periods which I have described has not been to reverse the premises of the dominant majority consensus but to modify what it believed to be the excesses or mistakes of the party in power, as it worked to achieve the objectives of the consensus.

This does not mean that the consensus which spread itself over the two parties has been impregnable or unshakable. On the contrary, it has been constantly dynamic and mobile, containing within it a wide range of divergent interests held in unifying suspension by a rough agreement on general policy principles and objectives.

Once the unifying purposes were written into the law and tradition of the land, these divergencies inevitably have been exploited and ultimately have brought about a general unsettling of the majority consensus. I must again point out, however, that these disruptive tendencies have not been set in motion by the appeal of the old minority to old interests, nor have they been politically decisive until a new dominant consensus emerged. Such a realignment of the groups and interests which made up the two parties has occurred only in response to dramatically changing problems either domestic or world-wide, which extended beyond the range of the old consensus and for which the old consensus had no answers.

✿   ✿   ✿

Now let us examine these features at work since Pearl Harbor, particularly as they affect our present consensus and the position of our political parties in relation to it. Such an examination appears important for two reasons.

First, a study of the limits and operations of our present agreement on public questions will help to free us from stereotyped notions of political alignments and issues, and permit us to look freshly and imaginatively at new political groupings which may emerge in response to new problems.

Second, we have thus far emphasized the fact that each new semipermanent alignment will be best seen in terms of its contrast to past concerns. Each new alignment was a departure, yet it took its *point* of departure from the consensus which was first recognized, then formulated, and finally brought within the focus of our political system by the previous political alignment.

As we have seen, it is central to the thesis that each new majority alignment does not represent a rejection of the doctrine and values of the previous majority but rather envelops them and goes on to something else. The Civil War was fought in the name of the Jeffersonian concepts expressed in the Declara-

tion, and the Welfare State was a modern reflection
of Lincoln's concept of economic opportunity and
growth as a prerequisite of freedom.

For purposes of more closely defining our area of
agreement today, as well as examining some of the
divergencies within it, I propose to consider domestic
policy and foreign policy separately. I make such a
distinction with reluctance, for all of us are increasingly aware that this separation is becoming more
and more artificial in the light of present-day lobal
realities.

Nevertheless, this integral connection between affairs which we usually think of as "domestic" and
those we call "foreign" was not so apparent in the
immediate past. Moreover, it is my view that the
differences we find within the present majority on
foreign policy questions are different in quality from
those which exist in the domestic policy field, and
are of vastly greater importance for the future. All
these factors, I hope, may justify my discussion of
these two aspects as separate categories.

In the previous chapter I suggested that the
domestic political consensus which has dominated
the past two decades has been in essence an agreement on the Welfare State. Our conception of the
Welfare State has insisted, of course, that the government assure certain minimum standards of individual economic security. In addition, we have
come to broaden the consensus, after some false

starts, to include the conviction that the government has a positive responsibility to adopt measures which will promote, insofar as possible, the full employment of the human and physical resources of the country.

Finally, as a corollary to these two points, we have come to recognize that the federal government must largely provide the initiative in discharging these newly defined governmental responsibilities, and that this in turn implies a so-called "big" federal government operating on a scale which was undreamed of twenty-five years ago.

To recapitulate, the current consensus which extends over a majority of both political parties, on what we may generally call the desirability of the Welfare State, may be broken down into three broad subheadings:

1. The responsibility of the federal government to take the initiative in assuring a minimum of economic security to all members of the population.

2. The responsibility of the federal government to take the initiative in promoting and expanding individual opportunities and the full employment of our people and resources.

3. The existence of a federal government with sufficient power, scope, and integrity adequately to discharge these two responsibilities.

In line with my thought that the decisive test of agreement is not what politicians say but what they do when they gain power, I propose to measure Republican actions on domestic policy questions against each of these three subheadings. On the subject of politics I cannot properly be described as a neutral, but I shall strive earnestly to be objective.

*   *   *

As this is written, we have had a three and one-half year period of Republican control of the executive branch of our government, and most of my illustrations therefore will be drawn from relatively current events. I will not, however, neglect the period of Republican Congressional control, in 1946–1948, for there, too, we should find supporting evidence if my thesis is sound.

Surely if the consensus which I have described did not actually exist, the newly elected Republicans in one of these two occasions would have put forward and executed programs and policies in fundamental conflict with those of their Democratic predecessors. · Yet the two periods of Republican control have produced no such phenomenon. To take this question at its simplest level: no New Deal legislation has thus far been repealed. Indeed, in the 1952 campaign Republican candidates devoted a major share of their speeches trying to convince the voters that any such counterrevolution was the furthest thing from their minds.

Not unnaturally, many members of my own party expressed intense skepticism about this switch from earlier arguments that the ugly blot of the New Deal must be removed once and for all from our national escutcheon. Had I not been in India, I might have contributed my own doubts from various public platforms throughout the country.

Yet in retrospect it is clear that the bulk of the Republican leadership had come to realize that the Welfare State was here to stay. The goals and programs of the New Deal had been integrated into American life. Although local contests might still offer profitable opportunities to some opposition candidates to support the old minority view, any politician running for nation-wide office from a typical state or district who bluntly rejected the basic premises of the New Deal was headed for defeat.

The same general conclusion results from a more particular examination of Republican actions in 1946–1947 and 1952–1956, the two recent periods of the party's ascendancy. Measuring the actions of the present administration against the three broad propositions stated above, I think it is beyond dispute that the large body of its proposals, and certainly those which have been successful, lie well within the area of compromise staked out by the present consensus.

Many Democrats may continue to suspect that acceptance of New Deal concepts by Republican leaders amounts to no more than lip service. They may assert that agencies such as the Labor Board or the Security and Exchange Commission, which are administered by Republican appointees who may not believe in them, are in unsafe hands, and they will certainly point to the favoring of special interests.

Yet, in the broad view, Democrats can take pride in the extent to which their ideas have now been generally accepted by their opponents. Instead of an effort to reverse the direction of New Deal legislation in such fields as social security, minimum wages, and the like, Republican legislators, many of whom still shudder at the very memory of Mr. Roosevelt, have agreed to modest extensions in several areas. Social security coverage and benefits have been expanded. The minimum wage rate has been increased. Support for public housing as well as mortgage insurance programs has continued.

President Eisenhower has even agreed with his Democratic predecessors that action is required in the field of health protection. The administration's proposals, although narrowly limited, at least recognize the principle that the government bears some responsibility in this vital area.

The present administration's farm policies have been under heavy attack. I feel that the attack is justified. Yet on objective consideration, not even here can it be said that the Republican party has challenged the *premise* of federal responsibility for maintaining farm income at reasonable levels. Although ample room remains for argument about what levels are reasonable and what policies will most properly produce them, it is an argument which one may hope can now be pursued with a sense of proportion.

In this election year most of us will exercise our right to criticize or applaud the efforts of the administration in the domestic field. But it cannot be denied that its stated policies and objectives clearly accept the first of the underlying premises of Mr. Roosevelt's New Deal: that the federal government is responsible for certain minimum economic standards for all.

*   *   *

THE specific proposals advanced by the Eisenhower Republican administration offer us, however, an excellent case study of divergent views at work within the generally accepted consensus. The Democrats, in the first two years as the minority in Congress, and in the second two years as the majority party, advanced counterproposals or criticisms of each administration bill. These counterproposals ordinarily called for significantly higher levels of effort or assistance than the administration was willing to advocate. The result was a bargaining situation. But as is characteristic of most bargains, the give-and-take was on matters of degree, not principle.

A typical example was the President's proposal for an increase in the minimum wage to $.90 an hour. The Democrats put forward a figure of $1.10 an hour. The political processes then became engaged both within and outside the Congress in the operations of bargaining and negotiation, and a compromise of $1.00 an hour was finally adopted.

The compromise itself lies within what I have described as the area of agreement or consensus defining the limits of modification generally acceptable to the public, including a majority in each party. But equally important is the fact that both the initial offer and counteroffer fell within this area as well.

I do not argue, of course, that the result would have been the same had a Democratic administration been in power. Indeed it may be helpful to consider how it might have differed.

I would assume that a Democratic administration's proposal might have been $1.20 or $1.25 an hour, and that the counterproposal by the Republicans, an opposition party under increased pressure to liberalize its views, might be in the nature of $1.00 to $1.10 an hour, which was the level of the actual

Democratic counterproposal in the current administration. The final compromise presumably would be
somewhere in between.

Now to several million low-income Americans a
difference of several dollars in their weekly paychecks is not a trivial matter, nor would such an increase be considered a detail by their employers.
These deeply felt interests are reflected in the vigorous reaction of both the Democratic and Republican
parties and on both the "liberal" and "conservative"
sides of the argument. But not even the passion and
heat with which the two groups support their positions can transform a difference of degree and emphasis into a difference on fundamentals. The minimum wage law itself is clearly here to stay, and the
rates are destined to rise steadily higher.

There is no doubt that the divisions between the
two parties in such a debate serve to strengthen already existing public impressions about their liberal-
ity or conservatism and the degree of their allegiance
to either labor or management. But it is impossible
to determine with any precision the extent to which
the positions assumed by the two parties on an issue
of this kind affect national elections.

Many observers, of course, assume that the practice of politics is no more than a kind of auction at
which blocks of votes are knocked down to the party
that bids highest in terms of the voters' immediate

and, for the most part, crudely material interests. This seems to me to be a vast oversimplification of our complex and interrelated political process.

Though the Eisenhower administration presents an instructive case study in the operations of the consensus, we did not need to await the arrival of a Republican in the White House to confirm the fact that, regardless of the vigor with which the phrase *itself* has been attacked, the *postulates* of the New Deal on economic security had become permanent features of our landscape. It was clear, I think, as early as 1947, when the Republicans secured a majority in both houses of Congress for the first time since 1928.

No piece of New Deal legislation, for instance, had been damned with more vehemence or ardor by the minority in the country and in Congress than the Wagner Act. By the tenets of the Republican diehards, here was Socialism gone mad. But even worse than socialistic, some insisted it was "unconstitutional." Clearly the time had come to wipe it out, root and branch.

Proposals which would have gone far towards this end were introduced, of course, in the Eightieth Congress, yet none of them succeeded, in spite of Republican majorities in both houses. The Taft-Hartley Act, which emerged as the compromise, cast formidable new obstacles in the way of union organization and conferred advantages upon management vis-àvis labor which had not been theretofore a part of the law.

One may argue, as I have, that these features are ill-advised; that strictures in the act make it unduly difficult to organize unions, particularly in parts of the South; that some of the "rights" conferred on management do more harm than good if our objective is a healthy, peaceful relationship between these two great participants in our productive process; and that these weaknesses in a period of depression would seriously threaten our economic welfare.

Yet it is significant that in the final analysis even those responsible for drafting this new law did not challenge the fundamental premise of the Wagner Act, namely, that labor should be protected in its right to organize, and that it should approach the bargaining table upon terms of substantial equality with management.

The second of our three subheadings of the welfare state was the proposition that the federal government is responsible for affirmative measures for the promotion of full employment of our human and natural resources.

Since the war we have experienced a generally high level of employment and prosperity without the special, direct government intervention which raised the blood pressures of so many Republican leaders in the days of the New Deal. One may persuasively argue, however, that such intervention has been avoided only because the Cold War has created the need for massive defense budgets which have given our economy as a whole a far more substantial boost than the WPA of Harry Hopkins and the PWA of Harold Ickes.

What, it will be reasonably asked, would the position of the Republican party be if this Cold War spending, perhaps under the pressure of automation, should fail to provide full employment, or if world conditions at some point should make such spending unnecessary? Would its leadership accept the need for greatly expanded programs of school building, city redevelopment, and foreign economic development, to meet these urgent needs, to fill the gap, and to keep our economy operating at capacity levels?

On this second proposition, it may be that the quality and strength of our political agreement has not yet been convincingly tested. We still hear talk in some Republican circles about the inflationary effect of full employment, and the corresponding advantages of four or five million unemployed to cushion upward pressures on the price level.

Yet the administration did not hesitate to act in opposition to these voices during the economic recession of 1953–54. The timing and tempo of its use of fiscal controls in general support of the economy may provide questions for legitimate political disagreement and debate. But it cannot be charged with denying the need for government action.

I find it personally inconceivable that a Republican administration would again permit an economic cataclysm even approaching the intensity of 1929. If such a catastrophe clearly impended, I doubt that there would be effective Republican opposition, within or outside of Congress, to using the full resources of government to cope with it. The constructive work of such groups as the Committee for Economic Development testifies to the now widespread understanding of the economic facts of life in our business community, as in other segments of our society.

Democrats may argue that there is a greater reluctance among Republicans to recognize the signs of such a catastrophe on the horizon and to move vigorously to meet it before it becomes full-blown. On this I personally concur. But this error, if such it be, cannot reasonably be considered a mark of original sin.

* * *

O_F course, full employment is only part of the broad objective which calls for the full use of our natural and human resources. Water resource policy falls logically under this general heading. Even here, where the pressure of private interests is great, a review of the activities of the present administration over the past four years indicates that proposals which fall clearly outside the area of general majority consensus have come to be so politically dangerous that they are usually consigned to impotence.

Our current consensus clearly assumes the importance of major federal participation in the process of water resource development. In view of this consensus, the administration is usually careful to cast its actions in this field, not as efforts to challenge the majority view, but rather as part of a search for a better definition of the *scope* of this participation, and the cooperating roles of private and state agencies. On those occasions when the administration has seemed to embark on paths which implied a repudiation of the *premise* of significant federal responsibility, its efforts thus far have failed.

I could cite the long and dramatic Dixon-Yates controversy, but it may be said that the circumstances of its unhappy end were too coincidental to lend much support to my thesis. I would reply that if my thesis is correct, the circumstances are not as coincidental as they may appear on the surface. Other administration programs have survived disclosures that were quite as damaging. Yet I am not confined to Dixon-Yates for support of my theory.

One recalls the fate of the first chairman of the President's Commission on Inter-Governmental Relations, Clarence Manion. This commission, let us remember, was created to do the basic spadework necessary for a redistribution of the federal government's functions which had been brought into being as part of the New Deal, and a restoration of some of them to the states.

It may be said that Mr. Manion's demise as a government servant was brought about by his politically embarrassing efforts in behalf of the Bricker Amendment and by his absenteeism. Yet I cannot but feel that his early speeches denouncing the TVA and bluntly recommending its speedy dissolution contributed in an important way to his departure from the commission.

Some will be ungenerous enough to say that Mr. Manion's only mistakes were in letting the cat out of the bag too soon, and in his failure to understand that the TVA may be easier to destroy by sabotage than by frontal attack. Yet I believe that this view would not reflect the situation accurately.

The like proposals of the Hoover Commission on the TVA were similarly regarded as quaint reminders of a bygone age rather than serious recommendations for action. Indeed, it is perhaps not too much to say that the startled public reaction to these features of the new Hoover Commission report has in considerable measure undermined confidence in its objectivity and competence and thereby damaged public acceptance of its recommendations in other fields.

*   *   *

THE same phenomenon is illustrated when we turn to the third area of agreement within our general consensus in support of the welfare state: the persistence in our economic, social, and political life, of "big" government. Here, too, in its early stages and under the influence of its less modern-mined wing, the administration seemed to move in directions which were fundamentally at odds with an acceptance of the need for a large federal establishment in meeting the demands and requirements of a multifarious and complex technical society.

The education program first proposed by the administration can be taken as an example of this approach. This consisted of proposals for federal legislation which embodied not so much a recognition of federal concern for our fast growing crisis in education as an effort to escape the responsibility that stemmed inevitably from it.

Yet opposition developed, based firmly on the majority-supported premise that this is a matter on which only the resources of big government can provide the necessary impact, and the opposition was successful. In this year's State of the Union message, the administration appears to have accepted the outcome.

Although many Democrats have been quick to assert that this is simply another manifestation of "leap-year liberalism," there seems to be little doubt that new programs which reject the concept of limited federal responsibility inherent in former recommendations will receive the support of both parties in Congress after some compromise about amount and detail.

Here again it may be appropriate to refer to Mr. Manion's Commission on Inter-Governmental Relations and to the Hoover Commission. Both of these trace their origins to the early days of the administration, when it was still the going notion among many Republican leaders that there simply must be some way to get rid of big government in times of peace. These two commissions were designed to point the way, the first by showing how great slices of federal functions could be returned to the states, the second by showing how other areas could be returned to the sphere of private business.

After Mr. Manion's departure as commission chairman, the work was carried forward under the chairmanship of Mr. Meyer Kestenbaum. His position as an important and respected business leader makes the findings of his commission all the more significant. They add up to the proposition, as I read it, that we have passed the point where a substantial reduction in the activities in the federal government can be achieved by transferring those activities to state or local governments.

As a matter of fact, relatively weak state governments, unable or unwilling to take major responsibility for economic matters, have been more a cause than a consequence of centralization in Washington. In state after state, the legislature is dominated by representatives from rural areas, while the people and consequently the major economic and social problems are focused more and more in the urban sections.

Although state constitutions, on the whole, are more detailed than the federal constitution, they are no easier to amend. Indeed, the state courts seem to have adopted a more rigid approach to the interpretation of their own constitutional limitations than have the federal courts.

As a former state governor who once attempted unsuccessfully to secure support for a modern constitution which would have enabled his state to carry a heavier share of the governmental load, I speak on this subject with some personal knowledge and conviction. As I discovered, the number of people with a vested interest in bad government is perhaps greater at the state level than anywhere else.

But quite apart from structural deficiencies in the states, Alexander Hamilton was right when he insisted that ours is a *national* economy. It may be persuasively argued that it was conceived as such at the very beginning, when the framers wrote the commerce clause into the Constitution. They foresaw that our economic life could not be compartmentalized — certainly not by artificial political boundaries. And they provided for that fact. Governmental responsibility for the fundamental health of the economy is necessarily *federal* responsibility. And the responsibility must carry with it the means for its discharge.

I hasten to add that there remains an enormous area of governmental activity in which the state must bear the major burden. The federal government has more than enough to do in dealing with the problems that are clearly national in character. Under normal conditions it must be able, for example, to count on the states for the maintenance of law and order.

This means far more than simply the vigorous enforcement of the criminal law. Under our system of government, the rules which govern the ordinary transactions and day-to-day life of Americans are necessarily established and enforced by the states. When shall a person be compensated for injuries which he incurs in a highway accident or at work? What sort of contracts will be enforced and on what terms? How does one transmit property? How do people get married and divorced? Who shall have a license to be a doctor or a lawyer or a seller of alcoholic beverages? The great difficulties which are created for federal interests when this state machinery breaks down or becomes distorted is forcefully illustrated by recent events in Alabama and Mississippi.

Nor have the states yet lost their capacity for fruitful experimentation with solutions to particular social problems, a capacity which Justices Holmes and Brandeis liked to emphasize. The problems of delinquency, mental illness, and health insurance, to cite only a few, immediately suggest themselves as promising subjects for such experiments.

Finally, the states provide in a number of instances administrative centers for the effectuation of federal programs. In these situations our system gains something from the fact that our states operate not merely as conveniently marked-off subdivisions of a central authority but as co-partners, junior partners to be sure, but nevertheless agencies having a tradition, a voice, and a force of their own.

When all this has been said, however, it hardly confirms the proposition that any major reduction in the burdens or responsibilities of the federal government can be achieved by transferring those responsibilities or functions back to the states. The present administration apparently has accepted the majority consensus that any such reversion at this stage is administratively, financially, and politically unfeasible.

The lingering hope among some groups that support may still develop for such a switch may be partially explained by the fact that it offers the one means left to the nationally impotent minority, which opposes the general consensus, to undermine these programs and ultimately to destroy them. The retreat into the concept of state rights by those who oppose the desegregation decision of the Supreme Court is a manifestation of this.

I believe it is sufficient to add that the Hoover Commission's recommendations to the effect that the federal government should cease performing any and all functions which might be performed at a profit by private agencies have not, as far as I know, been given serious consideration by any important segment in either political party.

But we did not have to await the advent of a full-fledged Republican administration to confirm our view that big government, for better or worse, is now a basic part of the general public consensus. Earlier evidence was provided by the Eightieth Congress.

One of the principal modes of growth of the federal government during the New Deal period was the rapid creation of administrative agencies. The story is a familiar one: in the regulation of securities, of broadcasting, of airlines, of trucks, of labor relations and the like, new administrative agencies were formed or old ones revitalized and expanded for the purpose of exercising rather broad powers over our economic life.

These new agencies promptly became the target of violent political attack. They were described as a fourth branch of government, unsanctioned by our constitutionally established tripartite division, and representing an unnecessary and dangerous expansion of the size, the powers, and the role of the federal government.

Yet when the Republicans gained control of the Congress in 1947, they did not, as might have been anticipated by their oratory, lay about them in wholesale destruction of these agencies. No serious effort was made to limit their powers. Instead, the Eightieth Congress, after some heated discussion, accepted the adequacy of the Administrative Procedure Act passed by the previous Congress, which was designed not to diminish the powers of the New Deal agencies but to regularize them.

In this legislation procedural conditions and formalities had been imposed upon the exercise of administrative power, which traditionally had been considered necessary to validate the exercise of any governmental power. Thus domesticated, the agencies were accepted as part of our permanent government framework.

These illustrations demonstrate the restricted political power of those who oppose a clearly established majority consensus in our governmental system. Their role is limited to modifying what they believe to be the "excesses" of the majority. In performing this task, the opposition can count sporadically upon mobilizing various divergent interests which generally support the consensus on objectives but differ as to implementation. Sometimes these may even be sufficient to give it temporary control of one or both branches of the government.

These differences of emphasis and direction are not to be deplored; rather, they are healthy factors in our system, for they equip the opposition with sufficient strength to help assure that the implementation of the majority consensus proceeds without unnecessary dislocation of other important interests. Enough has been said, however, to suggest that whenever the opposition tries to turn these differences of emphasis and degree into differences in kind — fundamental differences of approach — the result is a repudiation of the opposition, no less effective for the fact that it is sometimes silent and unconscious.

In the presidential election of 1948, after their smashing victory in 1946, many Republican leaders could not refrain from reverting to the anti–New Deal oratory of earlier years. That section of the majority which had deserted the Democrats in the 1946 Congressional elections, partly out of boredom with long years of Democratic rule and partly as a

protest against wartime annoyances, promptly took
fright and threw its support behind Harry Truman,
whose persistent political strength stems from the
fact that he has never doubted for an instant precisely what the Welfare State consensus wants and
how to get it.

❊   ❊   ❊

THUS far we have been talking
about agreement on domestic policy. Let us turn
now in my rather arbitrary division to questions of
foreign policy. We may be aided here by dividing
this category into two subpropositions, upon each
of which, I suggest, we have achieved a measure
of rough agreement.

The first is the necessity for cooperation with
like-minded foreign nations to protect our own national interests throughout the world. This has often
been termed a repudiation of our isolationist background.

The second is the recognition that in our modern
world the existence of a totalitarian power control-
ling major resources of territory and population
threatens our interests in the long run, and that the
expansion of such a power must be resisted and
thwarted.

The emergence of a general agreement based on

these two simple propositions is often summed up in what is by now becoming a dangerously multi-purpose cliché: "bipartisan foreign policy."

No one knows whether the series of close congressional divisions in the years just before Pearl Harbor reflected a deep division in the country at large or simply confusion over new and complex issues. In the 1940 campaign both candidates were sufficiently uncertain to play it safe. Mr. Roosevelt felt it was necessary to match Mr. Wilkie's promise that American troops would not be sent to fight on foreign soil.

Whatever the underlying public attitude, the sharp lines which had divided the Congress in the late '30's and at the beginning of the '40's were shattered with the explosions at Pearl Harbor. General support of a war effort may be accepted as a normal patriotic response, which does not necessarily reflect the more persistent realities of public opinion. Yet it takes more than war-bred patriotism to explain the sweeping public approval underlying our decision to play the leading role in the organization of the United Nations. Despite a decade of disappointments and frustration and an extremely articulate opposition, our commitment to this international organization remains, as I judge it, firm.

Nor can we question the massive public support behind the major foreign policy moves taken by the last Democratic administration in Europe. In no sense do I minimize the crucial support of Senator Vandenberg and his Republican colleagues when I note that they did not fly in the face of public opinion, but rather moved to implement its mandate in the face of Senator Taft.

The scope and depth of the broad agreement on these questions is manifested not only in the congressional votes of the Republican members but also in the distinguished roster of Republican names who bore a major share of the responsibility for the execution and administration of these policies.

When we turn again to the foreign policy record of the Republican administration since 1952, an appraisal of *acts* rather than words makes it clear that the basic policies forged in the immediate postwar period under the Democratic administration remain largely unchanged.

Considerable ingenuity, I am bound to say, has been expended in trying to make this continuation of old policies appear to be something different by calling it something different. The phrases which have been concocted to serve this purpose have become familiar: "the painless liberation of the satellites"; "the unleashing of Chiang"; "the New Look"; "massive retaliation"; "agonizing reappraisal"; and more recently, "the art of going to the brink"; and the "Reds are on the run."

Some insist that we can afford to put up with this political *sloganizing* in foreign policy. After all, they say, the Republic has thus far survived similar sloganizing on domestic policy questions. Our political ground rules, it must be admitted, give a fairly loose rein to such extravagances and exaggerations, and by and large both the parties and the public understand them.

Foreigners, however, cannot reasonably be expected to play by American ground rules, and in foreign policy, we deal with foreigners. These calculated phrases, in my judgment, have cost us dear throughout the world — far more than we can easily afford. But for the purposes of this discussion the pertinent point is that none of them have succeeded in changing the fact that the basic foreign objectives of the Truman administration are still being sought by its successor.

Here, as in the case of domestic policy, I do not suggest that there are not significant divergencies within the majority consensus. In recent months many members of both parties have become aware that the foreign policies, with their special European focus, which have served us since 1947 are no longer adequate to the global problems which now confront us. Those Democrats who share this view will move increasingly to the attack, while Republicans of similar persuasion will remain uncomfortably silent for fear of rocking the administration's boat in an election year.

When the sound and fury of the campaign have

died away it will be seen that these differences in view have far greater implications for the future than have the corresponding differences which we found in the broad public consensus on domestic policy. New developments in the nature of our relationship to the world and to the communist challenge itself are, I believe, beginning to undermine the unifying bonds which hold this divergent consensus together and to set up distinctions among its members which are beginning to gather force.

I shall return in the final chapter to a more detailed discussion of these forces and the profoundly important influence they may have on the future of our two political parties.

*   *   *

A CANVASS of the record of the current Republican administration such as we have undertaken shows quite clearly, I think, that at present the differences which separate the two parties on currently debated issues of either domestic or foreign policy are largely of degree and not of principle. It is a fair inference from this that the remaining differences between the constituencies of the parties and their respective voting support are of a similar nature.

Recognition of this phenomenon by politicians is

expressed in such formulas as "conservative-liberal-ism," "moderation," "dynamic conservatism," or "middle of the road." Obviously these formulas carry no meaning except with reference to a standard. The standard to which they tacitly refer, I suggest, is the continuing majority consensus in some such form as I have described it, which is recognized and accepted by most professionals in both parties as the present governing force in the nation.

In the absence of some *massive shock* to our sense of security which would upset our present political equilibrium, this little study of our political history, as confirmed by the events of the last four years, would lead us to expect in the immediate future a somewhat more frequent alternation of the presidency between the two parties than we have had between 1932 and 1952, when the Democratic claim to represent the consensus was largely unchallenged, and a series of close party divisions in Congress.

Yet these fluctuations will result not because of a bitter conflict over "the issues," but because the questions which remain to be settled have become less and less relevant as far as the voters are concerned. In such a situation the personalities of the candidates, the effectiveness of party organization, the size of party budgets, the skill or lack of it in campaign tactics, and various local considerations are bound to come much more fully into play in deciding national election contests.

The Democratic party may be expected to maintain the edge in these fluctuations from election to election. Some Democrats will argue that this is because their party supports the inherently more enlightened side of most of the issues which remain to be negotiated. Others may expect the Democrats to win more often than they lose, as long as the present majority alignment survives, because since 1932 their party has been the principal political instrument of what has now become the dominant view of both parties, and hence is more likely to be trusted by the voters to insist on its vigorous implementation.

The evidence drawn from an examination of the first Republican administration in twenty years demonstrates that this administration marks not the *achievement* of agreement among the rank and file of the two parties, which in reality occurred some years ago, but merely its belated recognition by the Republican leadership. I have tried to suggest that however reluctant and unconscious it may have been, this acceptance of the New Deal by the Republican leadership became evident almost a decade before, in the gingerly way in which the Republican Eightieth Congress approached questions on which its members had appeared adamant before gaining power.

Although this Congress failed to deal in any significant way with many domestic problems of consequence, we have seen that such political immobilization is inherent in the nature of any opposition party in our system. In this sense, the tag "do-nothing" was not so much an epithet as a destiny.

We can also find confirmation of the theory of a long-existent consensus among the rank and file of both parties by noting the Republican presidential nominees since 1936. In that year Landon was sold to the Republican convention as a liberal from Kansas, although his later campaign speeches scarcely bore out the advance notices. Willkie, Dewey, and Eisenhower are commonly viewed as modern-minded Republicans who seem to represent in their personal convictions a position that lies generally within the area of consensus which I have described.

But the control of the Republican party machinery during this period remained firmly in the hands of men of quite different convictions. And this, too, is characteristic of our system. The only members of the anticonsensus group who can get consistently re-elected to state and national office come from geographic areas where the national consensus does not prevail, where the national minority is a local majority.

Thus these men represent districts which *do not accept* the majority consensus, and, on the whole, they themselves do not accept it. But because they have a national platform, and because the seniority system in Congress often gives them a dominant role in committee work, these are the men most likely to gain control of the opposition party machinery.

Although they have not hesitated to exercise their power over many aspects of Republican party policy, these men have not been quite able to enforce their wishes as to the presidential nominee of their party. Despite their stubborn opposition at the national conventions, the party has consistently turned to presidential candidates who accepted or appeared to accept the majority consensus.

These facts alone, I think, testify to the strength and persistence of the domestic consensus which started to develop in the early 1930's, in response to startling new questions raised by the Great Depression, and which found its most articulate and ablest spokesman in Franklin D. Roosevelt.

*   *   *

IT is obvious and indeed necessary to the process I have been describing that significant differences of emphasis between the minority and the majority and their respective political parties remain. The two parties will undoubtedly continue to maintain characteristically different approaches that are conditioned by their history and by the deeply rooted positions which they took and bitterly defended during the period when the pres-

ent welfare state consensus was being developed as
a basis for public policy.

These differences are worthy of vigorous and
searching debate. The questions which remain out-
standing are serious ones, and most Americans have
an important stake in their solution. This is true not
only in respect to content but to administration and
problems of integrity in government.

But once we recognize that these issues are no
longer *central to our fate,* the political arena will be
left open for the critical new questions with which
we will surely be called upon to cope, questions
which already cry for debate and perhaps ultimately
a basic political realignment. Once the explosive
ideological trappings of the New Deal have faded,
our remaining differences of emphasis and degree —
differences which will linger with us for the rest
of our history — will themselves be easier to handle.

There is one further comment that suggests itself
before I leave this phase of our discussion. Ours is
not the only country plagued by a vast lack of proportion between the scale of political combat and
the prize that is being contested. Closely divided,
immobilized governments and hamstrung executives
are the symptoms of a disease endemic to the great
democracies of the West. Some have even thought
it a fatal disease, while others have attributed it to
a tragic flaw in democracy itself.

May it not be, however, that these symptoms are

traceable abroad to the same causes as at home, not to irreconcilable division or confusion or deadly paralysis of democracy, but to broad agreement on the day-to-day questions over which the political parties appear to be contending against the ominous background of world crisis, and a resulting sense of the irrelevance of the contest?

I put this as a question and not as an assertion. I am no student of these matters and one is always on unsafe ground when talking about the mechanics and dynamics of political systems other than one's own.

Yet it does seem to me that many of the distressing phenomena which we see in the Western democracies may be accounted for in terms of this same condition, expressing itself in ways dictated by the varying history, traditions, and governmental structures of the several nations.

Each of these democracies has passed through the battle for the Welfare State. In each it has been won, although in some cases, such as France, the result is not nearly so happy as we have had. Today their peoples are looking for answers to new questions, evolving out of what may be the greatest crisis in the history of Western civilization, while their political leaders continue to offer them the now empty phrases which were the fighting words of an earlier day.

May this not account for the frustrated vacillation of British governments since 1950? Or, in France, both for the increasing impotence of the parties committed to parliamentary government and for the growing strength of those which are not?

These phenomena are no less unfortunate because we ascribe them to one cause rather than another. But I am firmly of the opinion that our difficulties do not stem from any inherent defects in the democratic idea. In other democracies — Germany, India, Israel, Burma — where there is basic agreement upon a worthy national purpose *yet to be achieved,* there is no failure to mobilize the necessary energies and resources through the mechanisms of democracy.

Whether the prescription is everywhere applicable, I do not know. I am convinced that the need for this country, however, is precisely this: to develop on the foundations of our present agreement a new consensus related to the world-wide challenge with which we are now faced, to forge a purpose commensurate with that challenge and with our powers to meet it constructively.

III

A New
Political Focus

I HAVE sketched a general view of American political growth, and examined in some detail the application of that view to the most recent period of our history. Let us now consider its implications for the future.

I must emphasize again that I make no claim for the exclusive truth of this approach. Yet it seems to me especially useful for the light it throws on the problems and frustrations of the intelligent citizen in contemporary politics, whether he is a Democrat or a Republican and whether he considers himself a liberal or a conservative.

To note the spread of political apathy and to lament it has become commonplace. This lack of deeply felt political commitment reflects to a large degree, I believe, the broad areas of agreement on major issues, which we have just examined. The more fully we recognize and accept that consensus, the more difficult it is to tackle the remaining differences with the zeal and the energy which our democratic tradition demands.

During the presidential campaign of 1956, in the area of domestic policy both parties will undoubtedly support with every evidence of enthusiasm a federal school aid program, a federal highway program, expanded social security, further slum clearance, a balanced budget, adequate military defense, the wise development of our natural resources, civil rights, and improved assistance for our farmers. They will disagree, publicly at least, only on the magnitude of these programs, the speed with which they are implemented, and the manner of their administration.

Some highly important questions will be involved here on which many of us hold strong opinions. But in the large perspective of history, our preoccupation with these issues in the crucial year 1956 may seem even more strange than the forgotten arguments that divided us in the election of 1928, when the nation was balanced unwittingly on the verge of economic collapse and the parties stood on the brink of a political revolution.

There is little doubt that lurking somewhere outside the present area of political consensus are perhaps the most formidable questions in the history of man, questions involving not only the nature of life on this earth, but even its continued existence. A brief review of the far-flung global forces which are now formulating these questions suggests the scope of the challenge:

Following World War II Western Europe, which has always been closest to us in its interests, traditions, and culture, has steadily lost its world influence and power.

The Soviet Union has emerged as the world's second industrial power, the originator of a new concept of rapid capital formation which may be ideally suited to the underdeveloped two thirds of the earth, and the generating and directing force in a powerful politico-military combination which looks on the United States as its adversary.

Similarly China, with its population of 580 million and its long and friendly tradition towards America, has emerged under a communist government from generations of apathy and impotence to become the primary political and military force in Asia.

In a single decade the nationalist wave in Asia and Africa has already created sixteen newly independent nations, with a total population of more than 700 million people, one third of mankind.

In Africa, the last colonial areas under European control are sorely troubled with political unrest and racial tension.

Through the development of nuclear weapons, both the United States and Russia have achieved the power largely to destroy each other and indeed much of life upon this earth in a matter of weeks.

During the next decade the United States, which has been devouring its industrial raw materials at an incredible rate, will become increasingly dependent for its prosperity and security on imports from Asia, Africa, and South America.

Following Stalin's death and the development of the nuclear stalemate, new Soviet leaders have seized the political, economic, and ideological initiative by launching a program to bind the peoples of these crucially important continents to Moscow and Peking by close economic and political ties, and ultimately to strangle our military and economic capacity.

Liberal democracy, the ultimate triumph of which Western leaders since the seventeenth century have taken for granted, is thus mortally challenged by a dynamic new social and political order equipped with formidable new techniques of education, economics, ideology, and technology.

Our reaction to this many-sided challenge has been so clumsily militaristic and unimaginative that 38 per cent of the people questioned in a recent poll in Calcutta, India, selected the United States as the nation most likely to start World War III, while only 2 per cent selected the Soviet Union and 1 per cent the Peoples Republic of China.

There is irony, if not yet tragedy, in the contrast between the issues which these interrelated forces are creating — questions involving no less than the survival or destruction of our Western society — and those which are likely to engage our principal political energies in the election of 1956.

This does not mean that an effective new majority consensus cannot be developed that is competent to cope with these questions. It simply means that they have not yet been brought within the range where the political processes which create such an agreement are operating. The attention of the political parties has remained focused, in a manner I have already described, upon diminishing areas of disagreement within the broad political consensus that emerged in response to the domestic crisis of the 1930's. Because of this failure to grasp the significance of the newer and infinitely more momentous challenge, the power and influence of America and its Atlantic associates is now in jeopardy.

The analysis of our political history which I have

outlined suggests that the creation of new majority groupings results from an awareness not of the error of the old basis of agreement but of its inadequacy to new problems. It is well for any political party to look back, to be sure. But this it not least important because an appreciation of the ground now firmly won helps to reveal the outline of the territory next to be charted.

If the line of thought which we have been pursuing has any validity, we should expect the questions that are being shaped by the world forces which I have described, sooner or later, to give birth here in America to a new dominant majority grouping under new leadership and with a makeup which may differ significantly from that of the present majority.

On two of the three previous occasions when American society reached a decisive political crossroads, the response was belated and consequently costly. In one instance the result was a civil war; in another, the well-nigh total collapse of our economy.

Yet in neither case was it too late for a perceptive and competent leader at the head of a newly dynamic political party to prescribe an effective course of action which enabled us to put the pieces together again and move on with renewed vigor to greater accomplishments. We must hope now, not only that our political response to these new conditions will provide the basis for adequate policies, but that it will develop before the questions which face us become unmanageable. Since the new forces which challenge us include the hydrogen bomb, this hope carries with it for many of us a prayer as well.

If such a response does develop, however, our political processes may yet regain that sense of depth and direction which inevitably diminishes in a period when a still dominant majority has begun to lose its momentum and its creative relation to the problems that brought it into being.

❊   ❊   ❊

I STARTED this discussion with a disclaimer of any prophetic gifts, and I shall not attempt to divine the makeup of the new majority and its time of appearance, much less the precise content of its base of agreement. It may be possible, however, to suggest some directions in which we might search for a political consensus appropriate to the challenge which we face, and some of the shifts in the present majority-minority alignment which may be required to produce it.

Each of the political agreements we have thus far considered has been based on an expanded concept of freedom. The consensus which carried us from Washington's day to that of Lincoln called for a federal government adequate to cope with the divisive forces of our expanding society and directly responsible to the voters.

The next political grouping, which created an entirely new political party, saw the elimination of slavery and the further broadening of our economic and political horizons within the framework of a laissez-faire economy in which industrial interests were granted a privileged position.

When our West filled up and this consensus was unable to provide an answer for the problems that grew out of the shift from extensive to intensive economic development, it, too, was dissolved. The present working consensus, which replaced it in 1932, insists that a meaningful definition of liberty must include a high, government-guaranteed minimum level of economic security and expanding opportunities for all Americans, with a privileged position for none.

Now it is becoming apparent that the rather exclusively national orientation of the present consensus provides inadequate answers to an utterly new kind of world-wide political, economic, military, and ideological challenge, not only to our national security, but to the principles on which our libertarian civilization is based.

We may expect, then, that any new majority-minority political grouping will develop around a different interpretation of America's relations with the rest of the world. In this sense it is likely to depart even more sharply from its immediate predecessor than the three which we have already examined.

For, as we have seen, each of these three major groupings has been primarily concerned with domestic affairs. Although our discussion in the second chapter showed that agreement on certain lines of action abroad was a substantial component of our present alignment, this agreement has been narrowly based and restrictive.

Indeed it is misleading to speak of the foreign policy consensus which has emerged over the past two decades as a total rejection of isolationism. On the contrary, I believe that our foreign policy and the generally accepted concept of our relations with the world is still deeply rooted in isolationist principles.

What we have done is to recognize the fact that physical barriers — distance and oceans — which formerly preserved our isolation will no longer suffice. Under the pressure of events we have concluded that we need allies beyond our frontiers to prevent interference with our privileged sanctuary.

The majority in both parties which has supported our foreign policies over the past fifteen years has thus far largely conceived of them as a series of arrangements which will fend off the aggressive and intrusive forces in the world outside and leave us free to work out our own American destiny in our own way. When it becomes evident that this series of political alliances and economic arrangements, which was designed to free us for our proper domestic concerns, is continuing to take a major and increasing share of our energy and our resources without providing the security which we have presumably bought and paid for, we feel frustrated and cheated and many of us embark on a search for culprits.

Now on this rapidly shrinking planet, which we share with the Russians, Chinese, and 1.5 billion other human beings, the traditional quick, total solutions which we Americans have always demanded in foreign affairs are simply not available. Not only is any such narrow objective for American foreign policy impossible of attainment, it is, indeed, self-contradictory. We cannot be in the world and not of it, no matter how great our wealth and power. Inevitably this must become clear to more and more of our people.

If we are to strengthen our national security, expand our influence, and play the role in world affairs for which our history has prepared us, in the face of the political, economic, and ideological challenge which is now being generated by Moscow, we shall need to consider our relations with the world from a far broader perspective. Out of this broader perspective we must hope that a new majority consensus will emerge which recognizes the fact that we live in a world that is a *community* and which is prepared responsibly to support policies which flow from that premise.

If this consensus fails to develop for want of communication, or effective leadership, or inadequate political organization, or for whatever reason, or if it develops too late to be effective, the implications for our own and for future generations of Americans are not pleasant to contemplate.

Elsewhere I have sketched in some detail my personal views on the range of policies and attitudes which might be appropriate to such an altered view of our relations with the world. There is no space to review them here. But the following allegory may highlight my meaning.

When plague threatens a community its more fortunate members, like Boccaccio's lords and ladies, or those of Poe in his tale of the Red Death, are easily persuaded to retire to the manor house. They can provision it as for a siege, strengthen the walls, deepen the moat, station retainers at the gates, and reach agreements with others of a similar mind to join in keeping the contaminated at a distance. Within the castle the lords and ladies may pleasurably and even usefully employ their time for a while in savoring the concentrated riches of their preserve or in improving its arts and sciences.

Yet their tight little society will find itself facing some difficult questions. How many will be admitted to the manor house and who are they to be? How high are the walls to be built and how fast? How many retainers are to be mounted at the gates? What kind of arrangement with and what compensation for those who man the outer barriers?

Each of these decisions is a difficult one, involving not only conflicting pressures on the emotions and sympathies of the decision-makers but nice calculations of risk against gain. For as the company is expanded, as more workmen are hired, as more retainers are armed, and more allies contracted for, the possibility grows that some of them may themselves become infected.

Moreover, each new person is a charge upon the limited resources which can be stored in the manor house, and if there are too many to care for, the supplies may not outlast the course of the plague in the countryside. And may not the workmen and retainers, if they become sufficiently numerous and assured, turn upon the lords and ladies and destroy them?

Since the original decision as to how best to achieve security against the plague was itself irresponsible, these subsidiary decisions needed to implement the plan will become steadily more difficult. No doubt there will be repeated assertions within the castle walls about the necessity of "preserving our way of life." But these cannot supply the overriding sense of moral purpose which alone can bring ordinary men consistently to subordinate their personal, short-run wants to the demands of a larger end.

Ultimately this program for survival will almost certainly prove self-defeating. The Red Death may himself appear at the feast, as he did in Poe's story, despite the care that was taken to exclude him. Even if he does not, the lords and ladies, upon their return to the wasted countryside, will find that the plague has eroded the substance and energy of the community upon which they had assumed their more favored position rested securely.

The second possible course of action is to seek to improve the public health standards of the community as a whole. This is by far the more arduous path. Pleasures and immediate advantages must be foregone in some part. There is hard, dirty, costly work to be done.

The first thing to be noted is that this cannot be done *to* the community or even *for* the community by the lords and ladies, operating from a position of lofty privilege. It must be a common effort undertaken by most of the community's members with all of the vision and vigor of a truly creative endeavor.

From the very outset the lords and ladies must face the fact that no matter how inspired their leadership or generous their contribution, they can expect little or no gratitude from the community as a whole. Indeed, as its wealthiest members, they will be looked upon for some time with continuing, although perhaps diminishing, distrust. Nor do they even have the assurance that their enterprise will succeed, for the plague may yet come in spite of all they can do. They and their associates can only know that in this community effort lies whatever chance there may be for life, health, and vigor; the other way, none.

However, if the chance pays off, they may find that they have achieved far more than survival. They will have forged the beginnings of a society in which everyone can live with pride and good hope. And they will find, too, that they have begun to create the machinery, the loyalties, and the confidence for attacking with some success the new and perhaps even more subtle and difficult problems that are sure to face the community in the future.

Yet an increasing group of articulate and thoughtful observers holds that if the adoption of this difficult and more positive approach to our present global dilemma is dependent on the workings of the democratic process in America and elsewhere, we must despair of it. The inherent characteristics of democratic government, they insist, make it impossible for nations so governed to choose the hard course. Those in power, in order to maintain their positions, must continuously cater to the domestic interests and whims of a fragile and shifting numerical majority. Inevitably these interests, even in critical periods such as this, will reflect short-term needs and desires which cannot be adjusted responsibly to long-term objectives.

With this dark and pessimistic view of the futures of free societies, I must dissent. For one thing, it reflects a misinterpretation of the democratic process which has enabled our American society to clear so many formidable hurdles during the 180 years of its growth.

❉   ❉   ✳

THE previous political majorities which developed in response to the peculiar demands and problems of their times have not been transient, short-term groupings. On the contrary, we have found them to be surprisingly solid, stable, and persistent, involving broadly based working agreements as to the nature of the major problems confronting the country, and readily responsive under able leadership to realistic modes of dealing with them.

It is not the failure of democracy as a system of government that accounts for our present narrow and inadequate approach to public questions. It is the failure of American leadership in political life and out of it to recognize the new requirements of our fast changing world, to use our democratic techniques to help form a new consensus appropriate to the new challenge, and to call convincingly on the moral resources of our people. I believe that the emergence of such leadership in America, and indeed throughout the Western world, will call forth a public response that will provide dramatic testimony to the continuing vitality and adaptability of the democratic faith.

There is ample evidence in our history that men do respond to the summons of moral as well as material interest. This was clearly illustrated in the character of the New Deal itself.

It has become fashionable in some quarters to regard the 1930's as a sordid period, when every economic and pressure group except big business was invited to have a hand in converting Uncle Sam into Santa Claus, so that its material wants might be satisfied in one way or another out of the federal treasury. Some Democrats lent color to this view by the stridency of their own appeals to particular economic or cultural groups. And some Republicans, once in power, have seemed to assume that the one way to stay there is to regard the electorate as so many blocs of votes waiting to be bought by the highest bidder.

I believe that this reaction misconceives the essential quality of the New Deal and the springs of its success. Even those who opposed it most ardently must remember it now as a period of immense enthusiasm and hope for most of their fellow citizens. It represented among other things the expansion of the American community to include not only businessmen and farmers but Negroes, workers, immigrants, the old, the sick, and the unemployed.

The trigger that released the enormous energies of those days was far more complex and deep-rooted than the thinly disguised glee of various pressure groups at finding their place at the public trough. Both in Washington and throughout the country, men believed that they were engaged together in an endeavor to fashion a more just social order than they had known before, and in that belief they found a sense of dedication and fulfillment and their country achieved a great national purpose — the conquering of poverty and the expansion of the American Dream to include everyone.

I believe that a redefinition of America's national purpose in the age of global revolution through which we are living is not only overdue but that, once articulated, it will elicit a deeply felt nationwide response which will cut across party lines.

During World War I our role in world affairs was defined by Woodrow Wilson and translated through a series of eloquent speeches into the kind of national purpose which is so lacking today. Americans in all walks of life responded with a dedication and understanding that startled most professional politicians and sent waves of excitement and anticipation into the most remote corners of the world.

The war was fought and won to "end all wars," to "make the world safe for democracy," to assure the right of self-determination regardless of a man's race or color. People caught a glimpse of something shining, and they reacted with a new faith in their country, their future, and their reason for being. That the opportunity was lost through bitter partisanship, unrealistic short-term hopes, indifference to military questions, and general political ineptness does not alter this essential point.

Our reaction to World War II was in sharp contrast. Here our national purpose was clear, businesslike, and largely uninspired: to defeat the Japanese and the Germans, to destroy the Nazi hierarchy, and to get back again to our comfortable, normal ways. When Churchill in the House of Commons said that the principles of the Atlantic Charter did not apply to Asia and Africa there was scarcely a voice raised in protest throughout the entire Western world.

Yet every time the American people have been offered some national, responsible, higher sense of purpose, they have grasped it and understood it. The Marshall Plan, at least when it was first announced, was not proposed as simply another exercise in Maginot wall-building. On the contrary, it was presented as a genuine attempt to treat the world we live in, or at least the nations of the Atlantic Basin which are historically and culturally closest to us, as a *community*.

And this program, almost alone among our postwar foreign policy activities, it seems to me, evoked a sense of commitment and excitement in the nation at large. This, I think, can be attributed to the fact that it did open up, however briefly, a new view of our relation to and place in the world. Despite the fact that subsequent events obscured this initial conception, and may even be said to have diverted the plan from its original purposes, it has never quite lost in the public mind the sense of satisfaction and even excitement which surrounded its birth.

Yet in the last few years our devotion to narrow military concepts of geopolitics and our blindness to the power of people and ideas to topple governments and to sway whole continents, has led us into setback after setback in China, Indo China, South Asia, and the Middle East. If we persist in it we may ultimately face new debacles in Germany and Japan.

This negativism runs counter to our long history of creative political growth; it ignores, moreover, the ideological realities of the world struggle.

The most powerful ideas and principles in the history of man are closely linked with the evolution of American democracy. Today it is *our* revolution for self-determination, for human dignity, and for expanding economic opportunities which is alive and marching in Burma, India, and the Philippines, in

Nigeria, the Sudan, and Tunisia, indeed throughout the non-communist world. If the leaders of America's fourth consensus but rediscover the mission of Jefferson, Lincoln, and Roosevelt, we will find that we are again in step with the world and confidently on the offensive.

*   *   *

In the administration of the Marshall Plan, with its many leaders from business, there is, I think, an illustration of how the make-up of the new majority supporting a more adequate American response to the world crisis may cut across the lines of the present political grouping. Indeed, since 1940 and the Battle of Britain, foreign policy discussions have disclosed a large number of businessmen taking positions which reflect a keen awareness of the close relation between the future prosperity and security of America and developments on distant continents.

In 1947, Henry L. Stimson wrote: "No private program and no public policy, in any section of our national life, can now escape from the compelling fact that if it is not framed with reference to the world, it is framed with perfect futility." This viewpoint has not been confined to the Atlantic Seaboard and Mr. Stimson, or to such headline names as Paul Hoffman, Henry Ford, and John J. McCloy.

The membership of the local Councils on Foreign Relations and other groups which are seeking to develop fuller and more informed participation among our citizens in foreign policy-making bears no consistent relationship to the present majority-minority alignment in the country or to political party preference. Public opinion polls invariably show that businessmen are now the most internationally minded economic group.

Indeed, the foreign policy views of many industrialists and bankers whose hatred of Roosevelt is still smoldering are now closer to those of Walter Reuther than to the Republican leadership in the United States Senate. On foreign affairs the new consensus may include some strange bedfellows.

In the course of the past three years, I have spoken on foreign policy before gatherings of businessmen, workers, and farmers in all sections of the United States. In one brief period, for instance, I delivered speeches to such politically divergent groups as the Economic Club of Detroit and the Farm Bureau of Vermont, two organizations in which Democrats are a rarity, and to the National CIO Convention, where Republicans are equally unobtrusive. In each case I encountered the same concern with the present drift of world affairs and the same willingness to consider a bolder, broader, more constructive approach.

What I firmly believe to be a growing but still unrecognizable and largely inarticulate consensus on foreign policy cutting across party lines, is further illustrated with a kind of poignant clarity for me by the political situation in my own state of Connecticut. Fairfield County in the southwestern corner consistently runs up fearsome Republican majorities. Hartford County is the Democratic stronghold. State-wide election results often tend to be decided by a kind of battle between these two areas. Yet on questions of foreign affairs, and in particular on the kinds of issues we have been talking about here, I can vouch from personal experience that the sentiment in these two counties is remarkably similar.

Whatever the make-up and orientation of the new consensus which the present situation seems so urgently to demand, one thing is certain: it cannot ignore domestic needs in the interest of a new-found harmony. Indeed, our analysis has shown us that no new consensus could survive that failed to include the positions won by its predecessor. A new majority that supported any weakening of the consensus born in the 1930's and consummated in the postwar years, which calls on our government to assume responsibility for a broad minimum of economic health and vigor throughout our society, would soon cease to be a majority.

Nor could a new consensus ignore the massive military-security realities of the present world situation, which have been clearly grasped by the present majority. A new consensus will recognize the need for a powerful modern defense fully adequate to deter any Soviet military aggression, while pressing for a bolder and more comprehensive response to the new economic, political and ideological challenge which now confronts us throughout our revolutionary and increasingly interrelated world.

Moreover, as Mr. George Kennan has shown us in his book, *The Realities of American Foreign Policy,* a healthy understanding with other people abroad may indeed depend to a considerable degree upon our continuing energetic efforts to put our own house in even better order and to keep it that way. Hence, to promote a viable free world with freedom having the breadth of definition which it rightfully deserves, we must renew our efforts to make that definition a reality at home. A new consensus based on world requirements will almost certainly include many recruits for this concept who in a different period clung to a laissez-faire approach.

Yet with all this, one may expect some of the groups as yet "underprivileged" economically or in terms of social status to dissent from an increasing national emphasis on economic and political con-

cerns abroad. There may also be resistance from
some people of old American stock and of moderate
means whose sense of economic and social security
has been challenged by the rise of vigorous newcomers whose families came more recently from
Europe; similarly, from those who maintain unrea-
soning resistance to the ideal of equal rights for all,
regardless of race or color.

It is difficult, for instance, to see how the young
students who chanted "Keep 'Bama white" through
the streets of Tuscaloosa could join in a political consensus which seeks a comprehensive basis for cooperation and understanding with the new nationalist
forces in Asia and Africa, as well as with the older
nations of Europe and South America. It is also
significant to note that although the South on the
whole has remained true to its free-trading tradition,
debates on the Reciprocal Trade Agreement Act in
the 1955 session of Congress showed some Southern
opposition to tariff reduction, reflecting the new and
not yet fully developed industrial growth of this
region.

On the other hand, such international-minded
Southerners as Walter George, Lyndon Johnson,
William Fulbright, Lester Hill, John Sparkman, and
John Sherman Cooper, to name only a few now
prominent in public life, will almost certainly support a consensus which more squarely faces up to
the new, hard, emerging realities in world affairs.

*   *   *

THIS sketch of the social and economic groups which may merge into a new majority alignment or dissent from it is necessarily brief, incomplete, and tentative. It is clear in any event that neither of the two political parties can in itself provide the completely effective political instrument for such a majority. As with the earlier shifts in basic alignment that we have discussed, a new grouping that is really adequate to the world challenge is almost certain at many points to cut across existing party lines and the narrower interests now reflected in them.

Because of deep-seated political habits, organization, and laws, which protect the position of the two established parties against newcomers, the emergence of a new political party as the Republican party developed in 1854 seems out of the question, except perhaps in the spiritual as well as material upheaval that might develop out of a nuclear war. Therefore, the new majority will almost certainly be based on one of the existing parties, as on two of the three previous occasions in our history when a new consensus was forged from established political groups.

Yet each of the existing parties has its own peculiar handicaps growing out of the nature of its internal divisions, its traditions, and the variety of positions it has previously taken. The irrelevance of most of the run-of-the-mill 1956 election arguments to the global challenge which I have described illustrates the changes that eventually may be required before either party can establish itself securely as the political representative of a new majority squarely based on a new consensus.

I hope I may not appear unduly partisan if I express the belief that the Democratic party is in the best position to meet these new requirements. Yet I cannot argue that this is a foregone conclusion. It may be worthwhile, for a moment, to examine some of the rigidities in each party which may interfere with the necessary adaptations.

In the case of the Democratic party, the question of civil rights comes most immediately to mind. Although the Supreme Court decision has already resulted in the elimination of segregation in several border states, it brought forth a bitter last-ditch reaction in many parts of the Democratic South. If the Democratic party as a whole fails to take a forthright position on this issue, it will forfeit the support of the Negroes who hold the balance of political power in many Northern states. Yet the pressure for compromise will be strong.

On foreign policy itself the party also faces certain difficulties in clearing its perspective. As Dean Acheson has pointed out, the Democrats bore the responsibility for the conduct of foreign affairs during the period in which our present policies were formulated. I think it is now generally conceded that in these last decades the party has thus performed a worthy service. Moreover, in its appointment of many leading Republicans to administrative and policy positions dealing with foreign affairs, it revealed a remarkable and early sensitivity to the very factors which are bringing about the new consensus.

But policy formulation involves responsibility; responsibility involves defense; and out of this complex evolves commitment and some undetermined degree of inflexibility. To the extent that these policies, whatever their appropriateness to the European crises which brought them into being, have become inadequate to a realistic conception of the world as a whole, some key Democratic leaders may find it difficult to muster enthusiasm for another bold reappraisal of American relations with the world similar to that which they supported with such imagination and dedication in 1940 and again in 1947.

Foreign economic aid may provide one example. Democratic policies, in line with the emergency defensive premise upon which they were erected, assumed that economic assistance to other nations was a relatively short-term measure. Public identification with this position on the part of most Democratic leaders who were associated with these policies is already making it hard for some of them to revise their views on this central subject.

Yet the Democrats as a party are far more unified behind the foreign policy with which we have been operating under both Democratic and Republican administrations since 1945, than are their Republican opponents. Under our system of government this is an incalculable advantage. The Constitution, and the Constitution in this sense reflects simply the facts of life, assigns the conduct of foreign affairs in the first instance to the President and his associates in the executive branch of our government. Yet Congress, both by Constitutional prescription and in practice, has an absolutely crucial role to play. Because in American politics foreign affairs have generally been considered secondary, except when our failure to cope with them plunges us into war, a coordinated effort by the executive and the legislature rarely occurs until situations abroad have reached the crisis stage.

Other democratic political systems have developed their own devices for assuring a workable unity. In Britain, the cabinet system does so by staking the tenure in office of the majority party legislators upon their continued support of the executive.

We have not chosen to use this built-in device for assuring unity of action because our own arrangements seem to us to have not only compensating but overbalancing values for our American situation as a whole. The consequence is that the President must look to other means to assure legislative support for his actions on foreign policy matters.

Where the situation is one of obvious crisis, there is little difficulty. The urgency of the need discourages all but the most reckless congressional leaders from assuming responsibility for frustrating action. But to wait for unity in our turbulent present-day world until a crisis is full-blown normally means that only a negative, reactive foreign policy is possible. This course is incompatible, if our speculation is right, with the type of foreign policy needed to meet successfully the comprehensive and unprecedented challenge of the Hydrogen Age. What is more, it is not the kind of policy which will evoke a really wholehearted response from a new majority.

What I believe this new consensus will support and eventually demand is informed, conscientious, positive action over a long period of time and on many fronts in the direction pointed by the conception of the world as an organic community, divided though it may now be by Soviet ambitions. This effort will call for the full use of our expanding material, physical, and moral resources on a scale which the American people have not yet contemplated in times of peace. Working politicians and students of government both agree that the initiative for such a national commitment must come primarily from the executive.

What is involved is not only vigorous *administrative* leadership in coordinating the policy and program efforts of the State Department, Pentagon, Treasury, Agriculture, and other interested groups, but equally vigorous and forthright *public* leadership in developing an informed public opinion in support of the administration's proposals.

But the President's capacity to act is drastically limited if not paralyzed when he knows in advance that proposals which are fully adequate to the evolving world situation are likely to precipitate not only a difficult public debate but a costly, deep-rooted, bitter division within his own party in Congress. The fact that he can count on a *bipartisan* majority will be scant consolation if the biggest part of that majority is provided by his political opponents.

When the Democrats lost control of Congress in 1946, the administration in effect received a vote of no confidence. Yet because the Democratic minority in Congress was reasonably united on the need for whatever program might be required to deny Europe to communism, President Truman could proceed with confidence.

The international wing of the Republican party, led by Senator Arthur Vandenberg, gave him the necessary votes to provide a dominant majority, while the neo-isolationist half, under Senator Taft, doggedly continued to insist that America should have no truck with foreigners in time of peace. The President's party, although holding a minority of the congressional seats, provided nearly two-thirds of the bipartisan majority which enacted the necessary legislation to support a bold, timely policy in Europe.

Although the present Republican administration is led by a man who played an important role in our international ventures during the preceding decade, it is forced to deal with the critical issues of our day under constant threat of the same kind of split on foreign policy issues which set Vandenberg against Taft in 1947 and which contributed to Dewey's defeat in 1948. If the President breaks with concepts which are clearly proving inadequate and proceeds vigorously to meet the issues that have been generated by the new global forces which I have described, the majority coalition which he could almost certainly command would largely be dominated, numerically and vocally, by his Democratic opponents. It is difficult to conceive a more unhappy political dilemma.

In an election year, such as 1956, we see the results of this inner conflict in its most disturbing form. Members of the administration do not deny in private the vast deterioration in America's position which has been taking place throughout much of the world. But to deny it in public has become a political must. An administration program that faced up to present realities abroad would split the Republicans just as the civil rights issue may split the Democrats.

This is neither the time nor the place to go into the roots and sources of this deep-seated Republican foreign policy division. Part of it can, I think, be traced to historical causes that again involve loyalties and commitments which have outrun the realities of the current situation. In part it may be attributed to the sub-surface operation of forces which are already moving towards a new majority alignment. Whatever the causes, it can be agreed that the division presents a massive obstacle that the Republican party must overcome if it is to offer positive and effective leadership to a new consensus in meeting the issues which we shall almost certainly face in the next few years.

✿   ✿   ✿

ALTHOUGH we have been talking here of the pains and difficulties of political adjustment, I would be happy to end on this note. For what could be simpler than to suggest that much of the gnawing unease and uncertainty that besets our nation in today's world can be dispelled at the small cost of upsetting the prejudices and settled habits of some of our political leaders? To stop on any such note of optimism would not, however, be justified by present circumstances. But before examining some special difficulties that must be met in the years ahead, let us briefly review the ground we have covered.

The theory of American political growth which I have outlined affirms that at each of the three critical junctures of our history a majority-minority division has grown up and spread itself across both parties. This new majority saw more clearly than either its predecessor or its opponents the true dimensions of the issues at stake and stood prepared to give consistent support to governmental policies adequately related to their new vision.

In each instance one party under particularly competent leadership succeeded in identifying itself with the new consensus and thus rode to political dominance, while the other party's leadership maneuvered itself into a position of vigorous dissent. This early stage was characterized by a fresh, youthful surge of creative political implementation, which was followed by a long tapering-off period.

During this second stage the minority party sensed the futility of opposing the consensus; and the interests and purposes which bound the consensus together, although not yet fully established, grew increasingly remote from the changing needs and problems of the country. Thus both political parties became preoccupied with increasingly minute refinements of the measures which the majority had enacted into law.

In each case, the germ of a new alignment was present and at work for a considerable time during this tapering-off period, before the essential leadership emerged to place the new developments in perspective and to reflect them in political action. In one case it took a civil war, in the second, a depression only less costly than war itself, to demonstrate convincingly the inadequacy of the prevailing viewpoint and to precipitate the shift towards a new consensus.

Unless I am seriously mistaken, we are now well into such a tapering-off period. Yet there is a critical difference between this and any similar period in our history: in today's world, as I have already suggested, we cannot wait until disaster overtakes us to forge a new political answer.

This hard fact adds a formidable new dimension to the political challenge which confronts our generation. In the two earlier cycles of our political evolution we waited until a developing crisis created a light so brilliant that the new or broader truths were no longer obscured. Our slowness in achieving the necessary new perspective was costly. But it was not catastrophic. In the Nuclear Age our problem is to achieve the essential clarification before our democratic society is overtaken by total disaster from which there may be no recovery.

One might suppose that our high degree of literacy

and new means of instantaneous mass communication would create a peculiarly favorable setting for this effort. If Jefferson or Madison could have foreseen a day when presidential candidates presented themselves in every family's living room and when up-to-the-minute pictorial news by radio, television, and newsreel told us how other people were behaving in all parts of the world, they would have assumed that democracy's future vigor and effectiveness was assured beyond all reasonable doubt. Since the average citizen would be in possession of all the facts, he could be expected to judge wisely between proposed courses of action.

But the Jeffersonian view of the democratic process implied adequate opportunities for reflective consideration and reasoned efforts at persuasion. Even more pertinent, it assumed that the questions for decision would be close to the day-to-day experience of the citizen. Through the three consensuses which we have examined runs the common thread that Madison so prophetically described as the shifting conflict of domestic economic interests, of which our people had on the most personal firsthand knowledge.

When our forefathers became convinced that opposing economic interests or outdated legislative concepts seriously handicapped their own freedom of growth and opportunity, they reacted vigorously. Whenever their viewpoint became that of the majority, new governments and on three occasions whole new political alignments inevitably came into being.

A new consensus will necessarily accept and vigorously continue the struggle to create rising standards of living and opportunity here in America. Yet the central factor which will distinguish it from its predecessors is its realization that freedom in this tightly interrelated world is becoming indivisible.

The influence of free institutions, revitalized and newly focused on current world problems, will ultimately resume its historic evolutionary growth throughout South America, Africa, and Asia, or it will expire everywhere, including its birthplace, the nations of the Atlantic Basin. Whether the demise of liberty as an important political and economic force occurs gradually, through communist strangulation from without combined with hardening of the political arteries from within, or suddenly in the aftermath of nuclear war is, for the long haul, beside the point.

This crucial fact is now self-evident to many American political leaders of both political parties, to newsmen, government officials, and to a large segment of our people. But will it become self-evident to *enough* Americans to provide the consensus necessary for a new orientation of our national purpose and policy while there is still time for positive and creative action?

If the forces which threaten the continued growth of the democratic idea were to embark on traditional, overt aggression, the response of the American people would be immediate and vigorous. But nuclear power has helped to make such aggression old-fashioned. Modern totalitarianism now seeks to expand by political, economic, and ideological as well as by military techniques, obscured by familiar and persuasive slogans.

The adequacy and timeliness of our response to this far more complex challenge will largely depend, I believe, on the development of a new or revamped political leadership that rejects the cynical assumption that in today's revolutionary world the interests and aspirations of most present-day Americans are restricted to larger paychecks, faster cars, and more garish entertainment.

The emergence of such leadership out of the present haze of man-made confusion is by no means assured. The Jeffersonian faith must now deal with a paradox: the capacity for wise decision may be diminished by the very forces which make the necessary facts more widely available, at a time when nuclear science has multiplied the stakes. Yet what other means are there for assuring that the consent of the governed shall be a vital consent, freely given, and not one that is manufactured or manipulated?

Here again the role of the President becomes crucial. He alone has the power to cut through the barriers of misinformation and confusion which make the formulation of a more positive foreign policy difficult. Through his press conferences and radio, television, and newsreel appearances he alone can bring complex and unfamiliar problems into focus and marshal public support behind the programs which are required to cope with them. When a President abdicates this responsibility for any reason, he fails to measure up to one of the primary requirements of his office and places the security of the Republic in jeopardy.

In recent years demagogues have used the new technology of communications and the new knowledge about the formation of public opinion to conduct crude frontal attacks on our civil liberties. These attacks have taken place under cover of the controversy over how to deal most effectively with internal communism. Natural anxieties about our security have been converted into doubts about the meaning, content, and even validity of our traditional rights.

It is a mistake to dismiss those efforts as the work of a few extremists, abetted by a temporary hysteria, or even to equate them with the witch-hunting efforts of the "Know Nothings" of the 1850's or of the Ku Klux Klan. The implications in today's world are far more dangerous.

The fact that our present concern over civil liberties in the context of the danger from communist subversion cuts across the lines of the existing political parties may make it easier to meet this challenge. On questions of civil liberties neither party has a clear monopoly of vice or virtue, of villains or heroes.

It is also reassuring that our concern no longer proceeds on the naïve assumption that our difficulties may be remedied by passing new laws or by mechanical tinkering with governmental commissions. Something deeper is involved, which has to do with the quality and substance of the consent of the governed as that consent is registered by the political structure.

Efforts have already been made by scholars of Harvard University to sample public attitudes and opinions on these questions. These studies, though necessarily tentative in relation to the deeper issues we are now discussing, showed attitudes on questions of civil liberties varying not with economic status, social status, or political party, but with the level of education.

If this is so, it gives ground for hope, as well as providing a confirmation perhaps unlooked for in these days, of the great expectations entertained for universal public education by our predecessors. It also serves further to emphasize the urgent need to improve as well as expand our sadly inadequate educational system.

But upon our ability to improve our political techniques against the background of present-day technology may largely depend our ability to discover in advance of disaster the underlying unities that we must mobilize to avert disaster in both domestic and foreign arenas. It follows, I think, that any effort to impose an election year moratorium on foreign policy debate would not serve our national interest, for it would further delay our already belated efforts to come to grips with the future. Our highest priority at this stage should not be a harmony purchased at the cost of discussion, but a calm, responsible presentation of whatever divergent views may exist among us.

The surging advance in communications and psychology, which our own few domestic demagogues exploit, has, of course, been employed abroad with great skill by leaders of powerful nations who have only contempt for the principles upon which a free society is based. Their ability to manipulate information and opinion has made possible the first effective, fundamental, *global* challenge to the premises of democracy since these concepts took shape in seventeenth-century England.

For three hundred years the democratic idea was everywhere confidently on the offensive. Before World War I the freedom and dignity of the individual was the accepted goal of all mankind and even the most reactionary governments were being forced to edge towards it. The national revolutions in Europe and South America in the last century, the reform movements under the Tsar in Russia, Sun Yat-Sen's struggles in China, the Congress party effort in India, the beginnings of the independence movements in Africa, were all taken in the name of liberal democracy.

In our present-day world this is no longer the case. Eight hundred million people now live under communist rule. Their young people are being taught that modern technology and Marxist political theory have made democracy more outmoded than the oxcart.

We must face the unpleasant fact that through our own lack of imagination and faith and the boldness of our adversary democracy has been placed on the defensive. To the bulk of mankind the inalienable rights which our ancestors proclaimed to the world are no longer self-evident nor self-validating. Thus their desirability has become a matter of moral faith, and their implementation a matter of resolute action on the part of those in all countries and of all races who understand their challenge and their promise.

❄   ❄   ❄

WHAT I have said here is, I know, far from providing any truly adequate answers to the questions which I have raised. Nor would an empty exhortation to enlist new recruits for the important business of political affairs provide a satisfying new point of departure. Most of those who read these words will, I assume, have already committed themselves to participation in the political processes of our country.

I have not attempted to minimize or sugar-coat the unique dangers which we now face or to simplify our difficulties in coping with them. Yet as I look to the future and consider the great human and natural resources which have already carried us so far, I cannot help but feel that we will again muster the vision to rise to this new and challenging occasion.

America is more than a complex of military power, four-lane highways, steel mills, and soaring per capita income. America is the culmination of the efforts of many generations of common and uncommon men to create a domestic society of expanding opportunities and individual freedom for all of its people. The entire rhythm of our history, as we have seen, reflects this constantly broadening interpretation of the rights of men.

The nuclear, global challenge we now face calls for no more and no less than a further bold expansion of these concepts.

Nor is concern for the welfare of others and an awareness of our stake in the expansion of liberal values abroad contrary to our American tradition. The fathers of our country deliberately intended that their revolution should offer inspiration and leadership to people on all continents. Jefferson thought that its impact would lighten the burden of man "over a great portion of the globe." Metternich, recognizing the impact of the American experiment on other people, accused us of "fostering revolutions wherever they showed themselves." At Gettysburg Lincoln spoke not only for the Union but for all humanity.

We have seen that Wilson's concept of the world as a community and his plea for self-determination of all peoples not only awakened new hope in Europe, Africa, and Asia but brought the largest political crowds in American history to listen to his eloquence. Roosevelt's Four Freedoms, however cynically they were greeted in Western political circles, remain a promise of human fulfillment to hundreds of millions of people throughout the world.

What is needed now is a bold reassertion of these traditional American concepts, securely rooted this time in political realities and supported by the power, resources, and conviction of our people and their government.

There will be no lack of political experts to warn us that the full dimensions and implications of the present challenge are beyond the comprehension of the electorate, and that the issues which concern us at election time will continue to be marginal and re-mote from the deeper questions of our time.

Yet we may take heart from the fact that the political graveyards of America contain the remains of similar prophets, who in earlier periods of crisis and challenge likewise chose to sell their country-men short. The single decade of 1855 to 1865 saw the death of one major political party and the consignment of the other to a minority position for more than half a century, because they failed to measure up to their age.

* * *

WHATEVER lies ahead will be momentous and will profoundly touch the lives of us all. This survey of American policies has attempted to look beyond this year of partisan encounter and to catch a glimpse of this hazy but crucial tomorrow.

In the din of the current campaign most of the questions and possibilities I have raised will be forgotten. Yet in the vision of a world of expanding hope and opportunity for all peoples, in which America will serve as a partner and even as an architect, lies the only salvation of a free people and a free society. In this Nuclear Age, without such a vision — the people perish.